# SEXUAL CONSENT

**The MIT Press Essential Knowledge series**

A complete list of the titles in this series appears at the back of this book.

# SEXUAL CONSENT

MILENA POPOVA

The MIT Press | Cambridge, Massachusetts | London, England

This book was set in Chaparral Pro by Toppan Best-set Premedia Limited. Printed and bound in the United States of America.

Library of Congress Cataloging-in-Publication Data is available.

ISBN: 978-0-262-53732-2

10  9  8  7  6  5  4  3  2  1

To those who have broken their silence.
And to those who, for whatever reason, have not been able to do so.
#MeToo

# CONTENTS

# SERIES FOREWORD

The MIT Press Essential Knowledge series offers accessible, concise, beautifully produced pocket-size books on topics of current interest. Written by leading thinkers, the books in this series deliver expert overviews of subjects that range from the cultural and the historical to the scientific and the technical.

In today's era of instant information gratification, we have ready access to opinions, rationalizations, and superficial descriptions. Much harder to come by is the foundational knowledge that informs a principled understanding of the world. Essential Knowledge books fill that need. Synthesizing specialized subject matter for nonspecialists and engaging critical topics through fundamentals, each of these compact volumes offers readers a point of access to complex ideas.

*Bruce Tidor*
*Professor of Biological Engineering and Computer Science*
*Massachusetts Institute of Technology*

# PREFACE

[Content note: this preface discusses sexual assault and consent violation.]

Shortly after I completed the manuscript for this book, the United States, for the second time in its history, knowingly put a man against whom there were credible allegations of sexual violence on its Supreme Court. The message is loud and clear: violating another human being, disregarding someone's non-consent, does not preclude a man—especially a white man—from holding one of the highest offices of the state. This is, of course, not shocking. After all, Donald Trump himself bragged about being a sexual predator, and that did not stop him from being elected president, either.

In light of such egregious abuses of power, it may be tempting to look at a book on sexual consent and wonder what good it does. It is not that powerful people, powerful men like Clarence Thomas, Brett Kavanaugh, and Donald Trump, do not understand that the women they are violating do not consent. Rather, they feel that their own desires and their power override any objections from women like Dr. Anita Hill, Dr. Christine Blasey Ford, and the countless unknown women Donald Trump has grabbed "by the pussy." What good can a book like this, one that takes sexual consent as its starting point, do in the face of that?

The answer is that this book is about much more than consent. It is, at its core, about power: about the blatant abuses of it by men like Thomas, Trump, and Kavanaugh; but also about its more insidious operations—through ideas and culture—that create the rape-supportive environment we are living in. It is a book about peeling back the layers of this rape culture and dismantling the power structures it is enmeshed in (patriarchy, racism, white supremacy, cisnormativity, compulsory (hetero)sexuality, ableism, capitalism) until individual consent actually matters.

The #MeToo movement is the most visible expression of this goal to date. Brett Kavanaugh's confirmation is a reminder of how far we have yet to go to achieve it. But it is also a reminder that it is a goal worth fighting for. And fight we will.

# ACKNOWLEDGMENTS

This book would not exist without the contributions and advice of a number of friends and colleagues. First and foremost, though, I would like to thank every single person who has ever shared their own #MeToo story, both before and after it became a hashtag; and every single person, too many to name, who has spoken out and written about rape culture, sexual violence, and consent, especially in the various creative, feminist, and activist communities I have found myself in over the years. Those are the people and spaces that have shaped my thinking on consent and inspired both my research and my activism.

I would like to thank my beta readers, Dominic DeCesare, Charlie Ann Page, and Paul Wady, for their insightful comments and for ensuring the book remained accessible to the widest audience possible.

Thank you to my editorial team at the MIT Press, Matt Browne and Anne-Marie Bono, for their support throughout this project. Thanks to my copy editor, Mary Bagg, for doing battle with the *Chicago Manual of Style* for me, and for engaging with the subject of the book as well as its style. Thank you to my production editor, Liz Agresta, for shepherding me and the book through the production process and going above and beyond in the face of technical glitches. Thank you also to the anonymous peer reviewers, who were both supportive and challenging, and whose contributions genuinely made this a better book.

I would also like to thank Anna J. Clutterbuck-Cook for letting me think out loud in her Twitter mentions; Dr. Jackie Barker for moral support, peer pressure, and judiciously applied cake; and Debbie Watkins for making some very helpful introductions.

Finally, I would like to thank my Patreon supporters for believing in my work and providing some of the financial means that enable me to focus on working toward a culture of consent.

# INTRODUCTION

**Content Note**

It is difficult to have in-depth conversations about sexual consent without at least touching on issues of sexual violence, and this book is no exception. It includes in-depth discussions of rape culture and rape myths, as well as discussions (though no graphic description) of a range of ways in which consent can be violated or undermined. Please engage with this book in a way that is compassionate to yourself and others.

**Living in a Rape Culture**

"Me too." Two simple words, stuck together to form a hashtag. If you were at all paying attention in late 2017

Please engage with this book in a way that is compassionate to yourself and others.

and early 2018, you will know that they stand for the ubiquity of sexual violence in our society: sexual harassment, sexual assault, and rape, but also related crimes such as domestic violence and stalking. If you haven't experienced any of these yourself, you most definitely know multiple people who have. The problem is pervasive, systemic. In 2001, the British Crime Survey found that over their lifetime since age 16, 45 percent of women and 26 percent of men had experienced domestic violence, sexual victimization, or stalking at least once.[1] These figures do not even account for those who have experienced sexual abuse and victimization in childhood. This is not a new issue.

And yet, prior to autumn 2017, you may not have known. The victims of sexual violence continue to be stigmatized and even blamed for the violations they experience, while perpetrators are rarely held to account for their actions. Across a range of Western jurisdictions, conviction rates for rape have been hovering at somewhere between 5 and 10 percent of reported cases for years.[2] The majority of rape cases are actually not reported to the police, and neither are the vast majority of other kinds of sexual assault such as groping, flashing, street harassment, or workplace sexual harassment. Where victims do report their experiences to police, the criminal justice system is not only woefully inadequate in delivering justice, but it can frequently re-traumatize a victim through the invasive nature of both investigation[3] and trial—a phenomenon feminist legal scholars have dubbed "judicial rape."[4]

When addressing the ubiquity of sexual violence and how our society deals with both perpetrators and survivors, feminist scholars and activists speak of a "rape culture." Rape culture is the collection of ideas, practices, and structures in our society that make it easy for perpetrators to commit sexual violence and make it hard for victims to speak out or get justice. Some of these are ideas about gender and sexuality (think, for instance, about how we tend to see men as sexually active and women as sexually passive, and stigmatize as "sluts" women who don't conform to this stereotype). Some are ideas about what rape looks like or about how "genuine" rape victims should behave ("real" rape is physically violent beyond the sexual assault itself; a "real" victim reports the incident immediately, and is emotionally traumatized—but not *too* hysterical). Others are about who we perceive a rapist to be (rapists are monsters who jump out of dark alleys, not college students, or boyfriends, or politicians, or fathers).

We ask what she was wearing, whether she was drunk, if she "led him on," making women responsible for men's behavior. We think of rape victims as "she" and of perpetrators as "he," ignoring the fact that women can commit sexual violence too, that sexual violence can happen between people of the same gender, that men and nonbinary people can be victims. We talk of "*rape* rape" and by extension of "not *rape* rape." We have more sympathy for men whose "careers have been ruined" by allegations of sexual violence (such as Supreme Court justices Clarence Thomas and Brett Kavanaugh, both of whom will continue to shape the interpretation of US law for decades to come) than with their victims (such as Dr. Anita Hill and Dr. Christine Blasey Ford, both of whom testified under oath and faced humiliating public grillings and ridicule).[5] Perhaps above all, we approach victims' accounts with a profound sense of distrust, preferring to think that "she made it up" for the money, or the fame, or for revenge. All of this adds up to the environment we call rape culture.

The magnitude of the problem, and the personal nature of it—how close it is to you, to every one of us— have remained obscured by both social stigma and the inadequacy of the criminal justice system. Survivors and feminist activists, however, have been talking about it for years if not decades, bubbling under the surface, attracting attention to the occasional high-profile case (think of Julian Assange, Dominique Strauss-Kahn, or Bill Cosby to name a few recent ones), until they finally reached critical mass with the avalanche of sexual harassment and assault allegations against Hollywood producer Harvey Weinstein in 2017.

Following these and a host of other allegations against celebrities, politicians, and other powerful individuals from all walks of life, the importance of consent in sexual and interpersonal interactions has become one of the key messages of the #MeToo campaign, alongside highlighting abuses of power and the need to support victims and survivors. These are some guidelines the campaign fosters: Make sure the person you are propositioning or having sex with actually wants to do this. Don't harass women who are clearly not interested. Don't touch people who don't want to be touched. Whatever it is that you want to do, make sure the other party or parties want to do it, too. If you are in a position of power over someone, do not abuse it to coerce that person's consent. And yet, there has also been a backlash. From random men on social media and high-profile politicians alike come questions like, "What, can't I even flirt now?," and "Do I have to sign a contract every time I have sex?" These, too, are expressions of rape culture.

So, if we have learned one thing from the #MeToo campaign, apart from just how pervasive sexual violence is, it is that we as a society do not have a clear, uncontested idea of what sexual consent looks like, and that we do not all universally and equally value it.

This book, then, tries to fill some of this gap by presenting a range of feminist ideas about sexual consent. It is, by necessity, a book of a particular time and a particular place—or at least with a particular cultural outlook. Its focus is predominantly on cultures we think of as "Western"—North America, Western Europe, and to a

If we have learned one thing from the #MeToo campaign, apart from just how pervasive sexual violence is, it is that we as a society do not have a clear, uncontested idea of what sexual consent looks like, and that we do not all universally and equally value it.

lesser extent Australia and New Zealand—and it seeks to cover a variety of perspectives, experiences, and knowledges from within these cultures.

We will look at how ideas about consent have historically evolved, the practicalities of negotiating consent, and issues of power. We will examine the role that popular culture plays in our understanding of consent. We will look at how knowledges about consent are developing and evolving further right now, and who is producing them. And we will try to imagine where we might go from here. While this book is designed to give you a good grounding in feminist ideas of consent and current debates, as well as some practical skills, it offers neither sex advice nor legal advice. It will, however, point you to a range of further resources that you might find helpful if you would like to improve your own practice of consent.

## The Radical Potential of Consent

There is a strand of thought within feminism that says we should do away with the concept of consent altogether, or at least move beyond it, because it plays into ideas of one party (in heterosexual situations generally the man) being the initiator of sex while the other (generally the woman) is cast as the gatekeeper. This reproduces, the argument goes, some of the worst parts of rape culture by making women responsible for men's behavior. It does not view sexuality as based on mutuality and respect between equal human beings. And it may even function as a fig leaf to cover up abuses and violations because "she consented"— even when consent was extracted under duress, or when the absence of resistance was read as consent, or when, for whatever other reason, saying no simply was not an option.[6]

Heteronormative gender roles and preconceptions about who does what in a sexual encounter are indeed problematic in precisely these ways. Why, then, a book on consent? One of the key arguments of this book is that the concept of consent itself is not quite as enmeshed in this framing as it might at first glance appear to be. Rather, we are increasingly seeing the emergence of competing ideas, definitions, and derivations of consent in feminist thought, and it is important to acknowledge and explore these to understand what they have to offer to the fight against sexual violence.

Focusing on consent rather than trying to completely reframe the discussion on sexual violence also makes sense because consent is an existing and reasonably well-known concept, albeit one that is contested and frequently misunderstood. There is a significant body of feminist literature on consent, as well as a vibrant ongoing discussion around consent that has gained prominence in the wake of the #MeToo campaign. Our understanding of consent is constantly developing, becoming deeper and more nuanced as these conversations go on. It is becoming an increasingly useful tool not just for the transactional management of our sexual practice but also for interrogating all the ways in which our culture supports and enables sexual violence.

These developing ideas of consent reveal a radical potential to it. The feminist theorist Carole Pateman argued in the 1980s that consent theorists (both in the more general political sense and in the sexual consent sense) have been doing their best to paper over the radical implications of the idea taken to its logical conclusion.[7] Because once you really start thinking about what consent means, some tricky questions arise. Is an absence of "no" consent? Is a "yes" extracted under threat, or through pleas, or nagging, consent? How about a "yes" when "no" is, for whatever reason, more difficult to say? A "yes" when we didn't know that "no" was an option? A "yes" when we thought this was something we *should* want, or *should* say yes to, or that everyone else does?

When we move away from looking at consent as something that happens between individuals in a specific situation and start looking at it as something enmeshed in social structures, cultural practices, and complex operations of power, the radical potential of the idea of consent becomes really clear. This version of consent allows us to ask much bigger questions than who said yes and who said

When we move away from looking at consent as something that happens between individuals in a specific situation and start looking at it as something enmeshed in social structures, cultural practices, and complex operations of power, the radical potential of the idea of consent becomes really clear.

no. It allows us to start exploring the social and cultural forces that shape the options we have, how we see ourselves, how we are seen by others, right down to our very desires. It allows us to ask what the conditions are that we need to create for consent to be truly free, and truly meaningful. It allows us to start dismantling rape culture in favor of a culture of consent.

# CONSENT 101

## Bodily Autonomy: The Principle behind Consent

Discussions of sexual violence and consent are frequently dominated by legalistic approaches, which in many Western jurisdictions have their roots in property law rather than the very messy, human lived experience of sexuality. Part of the reason for this is that the law, and how it defines rape and consent, reflects cultural attitudes and practices and is, to some extent, *constitutive* of those practices: it shapes how we think about and express our sexuality. In this chapter, we will explore a range of approaches to consent, as well as how it is affected by rape culture and the law. First, though, it is worth taking a step back and elaborating the key principle that a feminist approach to sexual consent is grounded in: bodily autonomy.

Bodily autonomy is the idea that you get to decide what you do with your body, what happens to it, who else has access to it, and how that access is obtained and exercised. And you should be able to make those decisions without external pressure, coercion, or others wielding power over you. Your exercise of bodily autonomy can range from the everyday (you get to decide what you wear, what and when to eat, when and how much to sleep) to your interactions with a wide range of social institutions and practices such as medical care (you should not be forced into medical treatment you don't want), reproductive rights (you should not be forced to carry an unwanted pregnancy to term or, conversely, be sterilized against your will), and even death (you should be able to decide what happens to your remains, including whether you donate any of your organs). The legal recognition of bodily autonomy is far from universal. It *is* implied or recognized by the courts in countries such as Ireland, the United Kingdom, the United States, and Canada, though even in those countries it may be applied selectively in both law and cultural practice.

## A Brief History of Approaches to Consent

Applying a high-level principle like bodily autonomy to our daily lives is not always straightforward. As a result, consent is very much a contested and evolving concept, and the history of its development to date is far from linear. Competing ideas of sexual consent have been co-existing and co-evolving since at least the feminist movements of the 1960s and 1970s. There are four broad approaches that it would be helpful to understand at this stage: the radical feminist approach, the "no means no" and "yes means yes" conceptions of consent, and recent developments that can be broadly summed up under the heading of "sex-critical."

The radical feminist tradition emerged in the late 1960s and peaked in its influence in the mid 1980s. It was primarily interested in social power structures and how they operate to oppress women as a class. In the area of sexuality, some radical feminists argue that sex and violence, intercourse and rape, are so intimately intertwined (both legally and socially) that it becomes difficult to tell the difference. Consent negotiation does not happen on a level playing field where both parties have equal power to say yes or no. Social attitudes and upbringing condition girls and women to believe that their purpose is to satisfy men's sexual needs. And even the way the law defines rape (both at that time and to an extent even today) leaves plenty of room for violence and force, constructed as a normal part of male sexuality. In this social and legal environment, it is difficult to tell when consent is genuine, free, and uncoerced, and thus it becomes meaningless.[1]

The "no means no" approach to consent emerged from feminist campaigns against sexual violence in the late

1980s and 1990s. These campaigns were prompted by a growing awareness of the phenomena of "acquaintance rape" and "date rape"—unwanted, non-consensual sexual contact between individuals who already know each other to some degree or who may be romantically or sexually interested in each other. "No means no" emphasizes the responsibility of men to listen to and respect women's expressions of non-consent, and not to pressure women further in the hope that they will change their minds. "No means no" also has roots in legal reform campaigns, challenging legal definitions of rape that require the presence of physical force or threat rather than simply focusing on whether consent was present or not.

The "no means no" approach is fundamentally different from the radical feminist approach, as it focuses on personal agency and consent negotiation between individuals. The assumption here is that women are free to and do say "no" when they do not want sex, and that this "no" is being ignored by men, who go on to pressure, nag, threaten, or even use violence to obtain sex. This does indeed describe a significant number of rape cases, and thus "no means no" is both an important development in understanding consent and a key part of dealing with sexual violence. Yet it is far from the whole picture. One criticism commonly leveled against the "no means no" approach to consent is its inability to cover a wide variety of situations in which "no" has not been said and yet consent is still not present. These may be situations where an individual would normally be able to say "no" or negotiate consent but is impaired from drinking alcohol or by being asleep, for example. Power differentials may also play a role in making individuals feel unable to deny consent, such as when someone in a position of authority demands sex from a subordinate.

A key insight that allowed feminists to expand and move beyond the "no means no" view of consent is that heterosexual sex in our society seems to operate on a "contractual" model of consent. The idea here is that certain non-sexual actions and cultural practices, such as wearing a short skirt, or accepting a drink from a man, are seen to generate a contract on the part of women to have sex—specifically, penile-vaginal intercourse—with a man. This "contract" is reflected in how we think and talk about sexual situations, and in how the law interprets them. We tend to think of women who wear certain types of clothing, or flirt, or drink alcohol around men as women who want *and consent to* sex. Effectively, actions that are completely unrelated to either sex or consent are taken as synonymous with an expression of consent.[2]

The "yes means yes" conception of consent (also known as "enthusiastic consent" or "affirmative consent") is a reaction to both the radical feminist approach and the deficiencies of the "no means no" approach. In emphasizing the need for a clear, articulated "yes," this approach seeks to address some of the gaps that "no means no" leaves. It puts the responsibility on men to not only respect a clear "no" but also to ensure that their partner genuinely, enthusiastically wants sex and is able to say so. In law, this approach is reflected, for instance, in recent changes in the guidelines provided by the Crown Prosecutions Service in England and Wales for prosecuting rape cases. Greater attention is now being paid to how the defendant ensured consent was present, with, in theory at least, less leeway for assuming consent from the absence of a "no" or from unrelated behaviors.

At the same time, "yes means yes" is a "sex-positive" approach. Sex-positive feminism seeks to reclaim sex as a joyous experience that can be enjoyed by everyone. In this way it is a direct reaction to radical feminists' bleak outlook on sexuality and sexual violence. The emphasis on enthusiastic, clearly expressed consent seeks to reaffirm women's agency in consent negotiation.[3]

Both the "yes means yes" and "no means no" approaches to consent place significant emphasis on individual agency in consent negotiation. At their core, they assume that we are all free individuals who at all times are able to exercise our agency without others exercising power over us; know and understand our own desires, and express them clearly; make ourselves understood to others, and in turn understand them, thereby reaching a mutual agreement through negotiation. This reflects the kind of neoliberal thought that has been dominant in Western cultures over the last forty or so years. Neoliberalism sees individuals as rational and in possession of unlimited agency, unencumbered by structural factors or power relations. The "neoliberal subject" (someone who is seen as the ideal kind of person according to neoliberalism, or someone who has internalized this view) takes responsibility for their own actions, seeks to better themselves, and has unlimited freedom and choice when it comes to different courses of action.

Yet when it comes to negotiating consent, these approaches do not account for a significant range of sexual encounters that are experienced as violations by individuals but would not be classified as rape, whether legally or under either of the "yes mean yes" and "no means no" models of consent. They leave a number of questions unanswered: How do our conceptions of ourselves, for instance, impact our decisions to consent to or even initiate sex? What does it mean to be feminine or a woman in relation to the choices we make about sex? What does it mean to be masculine or a man? What do our ideas about virginity or marriage tell us about how we should conduct our sexual and romantic relationships? How about ideas of what counts as sex, who should be having sex, what a "normal" amount of sex is? Our society has a lot of dominant ideas about sexuality, many or all of which we internalize, and which then shape our choices and actions.

As a result, some feminists have more recently returned to some of the questions raised by radical feminist approaches about issues of structures and power imbalances as they relate to consent negotiation. This has led to the development of a variety of "sex-critical" approaches to consent.[4] Like radical feminist approaches, these pay attention to issues of power in consent negotiation. But sex-critical feminists also tend to have a more nuanced conception of power, not as a monolithic, top-down oppressive force, but as an interaction of multiple forces, all pushing in different directions. Many of these approaches put less emphasis on legal frameworks and more on the role of culture (both in the sense of popular culture and in the sense of our everyday practices) in creating the conditions under which sexual violence thrives and the conditions for tackling it.

A key insight can be gained from these sex-critical approaches, and it has implications for our thinking on consent. We can see the seeds of this idea in the contractual model of consent: that linear progression identified in the contractual model, from wearing a short skirt to having a few drinks to intercourse, can be thought of as a script—a set and progression of actions and behaviors we can easily follow. And that progression is by far the most dominant sexual script in our society. It shapes the way we think about what sex is (penile-vaginal intercourse), who has sex (exactly one non-disabled cisgender man and one non-disabled cisgender woman), and as a result what actions might require consent (intercourse) and what actions might constitute or be read as consent (following that script right up to intercourse).

Sex-critical approaches to consent recognize these cultural practices and dominant ideas as something that may shape our thoughts and actions, and may constrain our ability to exercise bodily autonomy. Ultimately, they ask what the conditions are under which we can *freely* say "no" to sex, as those are also the conditions under which our "yes" becomes truly meaningful.

## Rape Culture and Rape Myths

The cultural practices and beliefs that sex-critical feminists have identified as limiting our agency and ability to exercise bodily autonomy belong to a wider "rape culture" or "rape-supportive culture." This comprises dominant attitudes to gender, sexuality, and sex that create an environment where saying no to sex is more difficult than saying yes, where unrelated actions are taken to imply consent, and the benefit of the doubt is given always to the perpetrator and never to the victim. It also includes a culture where not only gender, but also race, sexual orientation, age, disability, and myriad other differences are wielded as tools of power, marginalizing

Sex-critical approaches to consent recognize certain cultural practices and dominant ideas—such as the linear progression in the contractual model of consent—as something that may shape our thoughts and actions, and may constrain our ability to exercise bodily autonomy.

some groups and making them even move vulnerable to sexual violence.

A key part of what makes our culture "rape-supportive" is an array of rape myths: ideas we hold about the kinds of people who commit rape, the kinds of people who experience it, what rape actually is, what a rape victim looks like and how they should behave, or whose responsibility it is to prevent rape. It is worth examining some of these myths in detail to understand how they may travel between our cultural environment and our legal system, thereby both reproducing rape culture and limiting our ability to freely negotiate consent.

Perhaps the most common rape myth is that rapists are strangers who jump out of dark alleys with weapons. In fact, the vast majority of sexual violence is committed by people known to the victim: acquaintances, family members, colleagues, partners, husbands. What this myth does is make rape seem like an extraordinary event when in reality, for many victims, it can be very ordinary and downright domestic. As a result, it also makes rapists seem like extraordinary monsters rather than the everyday people they actually are. The practice, still common in some jurisdictions, of calling character witnesses to speak in favor of the defendant in rape trials reflects this rape myth and shows the damage it does to victims' prospects of getting justice. Ultimately, this myth detracts from both the importance and the complexity of consent by suggesting that only one type of rape exists, and that it is obvious when that has occurred.

Another common myth is that rape always involves other types of physical violence. This myth conflates sexual violence with other physical violence, thereby dismissing all the cases of rape, sexual assault, and boundary and consent violations where the victim does not sustain other visible injuries. Where the stranger rape myth suggests that we can tell if it was a rape from the circumstances and the relationship between victim and perpetrator, the violent rape myth suggests that we can tell whether rape allegations are true from the physical state of the victim, again detracting from the core question of consent.

The idea that women always put up token resistance to sex, but in reality they want it, is another pervasive rape myth. It works side by side with the myth that unless a woman put up the *utmost resistance* (screamed, kicked, fought, tried to run away, and sustained other physical injuries in the process), she consented. These two myths cast women's expressions of consent and non-consent as ambiguous and untrustworthy. They give rapists permission to ignore a first (and second, and third) no, to keep pushing and violating boundaries until they get what they want. They allow rape complaints to be dismissed and victims to be blamed for not resisting vigorously enough. They ignore the realities of rape experiences: that victims freeze, especially when assaulted by someone they know and trust; that fighting back puts them at greater risk of additional injuries; that rapists use intimidation and manipulation more than physical violence.

Another set of common myths is that women provoke rape by wearing revealing clothing, drinking too much to be able to protect themselves, or walking alone after dark and that, conversely, men can't help themselves when provoked in these ways. These myths mean that for women, drinking too much is reason to blame them, but for men it is reason to excuse their behavior. They function to move responsibility from rapists to victims. Rather than saying to potential perpetrators, "Don't rape," they tell potential victims, "Don't get raped." They limit women's ability to move freely in public spaces or dress the way they want. Fundamentally, these myths suggest that indications of consent are not to be found in what a woman says in a potentially sexual situation, but in her actions in entirely unrelated situations.

Rape culture does not affect us all equally. There are myths about specific, marginalized groups that make them even more vulnerable in this environment of pervasive sexual violence. There is, for instance, a myth that sex workers cannot be raped—that the nature of their work means they waive the right to withhold consent. This is untrue: sex workers have the same right to bodily autonomy that anyone else has. Yet this myth is widespread in culture as well as in the criminal justice system and other support services, and this is one of the factors that expose sex workers to greater risk of sexual assault.

The racialization of some groups—their construction as "other" based on skin color or origin—also significantly contributes to rape culture and the marginalization of racialized groups. The United States, for instance, has a long cultural history of conceptualizing rape as a crime perpetrated predominantly by black men against white women.[5] This construction is part of a deliberate effort to reframe and erase a history of white men raping enslaved black women and indigenous women, and it has profoundly oppressive effects on black and indigenous women to this day. Black and indigenous women experience sexual violence at much greater rates than white women. These cultural myths carry over into the criminal justice system, as both black and indigenous women are less likely to be believed when they report sexual assault, and they are less likely to have their cases taken further by investigators and prosecutors. Similar myths also operate to render other women of color more vulnerable to sexual violence.[6]

These myths, and other, more subtle ones, are widespread in our culture, both in how we think about issues of sex and sexual violence on a day-to-day basis and in how these issues and sexuality more generally are represented in popular culture. They function to deflect blame and responsibility for sexual violence from those who perpetrate it to its victims. They play a significant role not only in how we as individuals relate to issues of sexual violence (think, for instance, of what your first response would be if a friend confided in you that they had been raped), but also in how our media and even the law treats the issue.

## Consent and the Law

So far in this chapter, we have only touched on the role of the law in sexual consent briefly and tangentially, but it is important to understand not only what the law has to say about consent but also how it operates in practice when it is required to intervene. This is because law—both as legislation and as it is implemented in practice through the criminal justice system—plays a significant role in shaping how we think about consent and consequently how we behave.

We tend to think of the law as a coherent, consistent body of rules that governs our lives. Yet this is far from legal reality. Laws evolve over time, are reinterpreted by the courts, and lawmaking generally involves compromise, which in turn leads to some interesting inconsistencies. Marriage laws for instance tend to view sex—specifically, penile-vaginal intercourse—as an integral part of marriage, and procreation as the main purpose of marital sex. This is why there is a consummation requirement for different-gender marriages in English and Welsh law, and why historically marital rape was not considered an offense. Even with the more recent recognition of marital rape as an offense, the consummation requirement remains, making different-gender marriage conditional on at least one instance of penile-vaginal intercourse regardless of consent. This discrepancy highlights the fact that the law is not unified and consistent, but frequently contradictory.

Legally speaking, sexual offenses tend to be rooted either in property law (an offense against your right to limit others' use of your property, in this case your body), or in ideas about public order (certain sexual acts are seen as socially undesirable and therefore prohibited). While feminist and queer legal reform campaigns have had some success in updating legislation, bringing it more in line with contemporary social attitudes, and eliminating some of the most egregious injustices, the law remains a blunt tool that does not actually reflect the sometimes messy experience of human sexuality, or what we as a society or as individuals may value about our sexuality.[7]

How exactly the law defines rape can tell us a lot about dominant social attitudes and their historical development, as well as our values when it comes to sex and consent. Legal definitions of rape and other sexual assault tend to start from the point of view of non-consent, and they do vary somewhat by jurisdiction. In the United Kingdom, rape is broadly speaking defined as non-consensual

How exactly the law defines rape can tell us a lot about dominant social attitudes and their historical development, as well as our values when it comes to sex and consent.

penetration of the vagina, anus, or mouth with a penis, while other offenses exist to account for penetration with objects or making someone penetrate another person. The Republic of Ireland has two rape offenses, one for non-consensual vaginal penetration by a penis, and a second for anal and oral penetration as well as vaginal penetration by an inanimate object. In the United States, the legal definition of rape varies by state, though there is also a federal definition for the purpose of crime statistics, which defines rape as "the penetration, no matter how slight, of the vagina or anus with any body part or object, or oral penetration by a sex organ of another person, without the consent of the victim."[8]

Canadian law is fairly unusual here, in that it does not recognize rape as a separate offense, instead opting for the wider category of "sexual assault," which is defined as non-consensual sexual contact. Like Canada, New Zealand also has a wider category of "sexual violation," though New Zealand law also recognizes rape as a separate crime within that. Through laws on sexual assault, jurisdictions such as the United Kingdom, Ireland, the United States, and New Zealand, which do have separate rape laws, also acknowledge that there are a number of other sexual offenses that do not involve penetration; these offenses, however, are in some ways considered less severe. This kind of "tiering" of sexual offenses, with penetrative rape at the "top," creates a structure that privileges some sexual acts over others, implying that some sexual acts "count" more than others. This reflects dominant sexual scripts where penile-vaginal intercourse is cast as the endgame, with everything else being relegated to "foreplay." We will return to the impact such tiering of sexual acts has on our behavior and ability to give consent freely in chapters 3 and 4.

Another key factor in legal definitions of rape is to what extent consent plays a role at all. Legal traditions rooted in English law (as seen in the United States, Canada, and Ireland) tend to have consent-centric definitions of rape; that is, the overriding criterion for whether an act is rape or not is consent—in theory, at least. Other jurisdictions (for instance, much of Europe) still require that additional conditions be met to qualify the act as rape—and they range from the victim being subject to threats or force to the victim being impaired and unable to resist. As a result, in countries such as France, Norway, and Switzerland, "no" does not mean "no": victims may have clearly communicated that they did not consent to a sexual act, but unless other factors were also present, their assailants may not be ruled guilty of rape.[9]

There is also the question of consent being extracted under coercion or duress: a person saying yes because they fear the consequences of saying no, such as physical violence or losing a job. Even consent-centric definitions of rape tend to be too vague to cover some of these eventualities. As a result, in legal practice this question is frequently left to defense lawyers who then focus on verbal and physical expressions of apparent consent rather than whether consent was freely given.

Even some jurisdictions with consent-centric definitions of rape have issues when it comes to what exactly constitutes consent, when it can be given, and when it can be withdrawn. A 1979 North Carolina Supreme Court decision, for instance, holds that once consent for an act of penetration is given, it cannot be withdrawn: a man is not guilty of rape if he continues to have intercourse with a woman who has withdrawn consent. While it is questionable whether courts would interpret North Carolina law in the same way today, the ruling has had an impact on prosecutors' decisions on how to deal with recent cases, and repeated efforts to clarify the law have failed.[10]

Legal definitions of rape and consent reflect and reinforce cultural attitudes and beliefs, and can have a significant impact on how we think about sex. Beyond definitions, there is also a significant body of feminist literature on the law as practice (i.e., what actually happens in courtrooms and other parts of the criminal justice system) when it comes to sexual offenses. Practices of evidence collection, decision making on whether to prosecute a particular case, and what happens in a courtroom all reproduce rape culture, re-traumatizing and blaming survivors of sexual violence while acquitting those who perpetrate it.

Legal proceedings have a special status in our society, in that their outcome, in the form of guilty or not guilty verdicts, carries the weight of truth, as well as potential consequences for the accused. For that reason, the burden of proof in a criminal trial lies with the prosecution (i.e., defendants are considered innocent until proven guilty), and there is a high standard of proof—the jury needs to be convinced of the defendant's guilt "beyond reasonable doubt." The adversarial trial system only admits one possible version of events, that of the alleged victim *or* that of the alleged perpetrator. The process of establishing that version can be deeply traumatic for victims and frequently fails to actually deliver justice.[11]

Rape myths play a key role in how the law reproduces rape culture. Studies of rape trials across a number of Western jurisdictions have shown how rape myths are leveraged by defense lawyers and rarely challenged by judges or even prosecutors. Victims, for instance, are frequently asked about the extent of any resistance they put up, reproducing the myth that anything but the *utmost* resistance constitutes consent. Victims' behavior leading up to the rape is scrutinized, reproducing the contractual model of consent and the idea that unrelated actions, such as how someone is dressed or whether they flirted, is a better indicator of consent than a clear "no." This interplay between culture and the law allows defense lawyers to manipulate jurors, introducing doubt that, in the context of rape culture, seems perfectly reasonable.[12]

Much like rape culture, the law also does not affect everyone equally, and marginalized groups are structurally disadvantaged by the law—the legislation itself and the ways in which it is enforced. In US legal history, for instance, women of color—black and indigenous women in particular—were not regarded as rapable. Rape was a crime that could only be committed against a white woman. And while the legal inequality has at least in theory been redressed, in practice women of color still face innumerable barriers to accessing justice for sexual violence committed against them. In the case of indigenous women living on lands under tribal sovereignty, a series of legal loopholes mean rapes of indigenous women by white men are under the jurisdiction of the US federal government, which declines to prosecute the vast majority of reported cases.[13]

Feminist legal scholars and activists across many Western jurisdictions have achieved some important legal reforms over the last fifty years, from the recognition of marital rape as an offense to improvements in trial practice, such as making a rape victim's sexual history inadmissible as evidence except in very rare and specific circumstances. It is notable that these reforms have rarely addressed the kinds of issues that disproportionately affect marginalized women, largely benefiting privileged women instead. Arguably they have also not led to either a significant increase in conviction rates, or a decrease in sexual violence. For these and other reasons, other theorists and activists have argued for the need to *decenter* the law in our approaches to sexual violence. Because the law is a blunt tool, seeks binary yes/no answers, and inevitably invalidates at least one party's lived experience, some feminist scholars and activists argue that it is not fit to deal with the immense complexity of human sexuality.[14] These strands of thought favor cultural change and the use of restorative and transformative justice methods over legal reform.

## Beyond Penile-Vaginal Intercourse

One common thread that runs through dominant Western cultural beliefs about gender and sex, legal frameworks on sexual violence, and particularly early feminist approaches to rape and consent is the assumption that sex—and therefore rape and other sexual violence—happens between a non-disabled cisgender man and a non-disabled cisgender woman. In this model of rape, reflected for instance in definitions of rape that focus on penetration of the vagina with a penis, the man is always the aggressor, the woman always the victim. The act of penile-vaginal intercourse is privileged, legally and culturally, as the one sexual act that requires consent.

This construction of sex and what requires consent has several potentially negative consequences, both for marginalized groups who do not fit the cis- and hetero-normative default and more broadly for anyone seeking to exercise their bodily autonomy and negotiate consent in their relationships. Transgender people, intersex people, those whose sexual orientations deviate from the allo- and heterosexual norm, as well as disabled people whose sexual practices may vary from the intercourse-centric norm, are excluded from the cultural and sometimes even the legal discourse on sexual consent and sexual violence. And if we conceptualize penile-vaginal intercourse as the main or only act that requires consent, we risk obscuring a whole range of behaviors that push boundaries and violate bodily autonomy. In the next two chapters, we will explore these issues in more depth by taking a look at how consent negotiation may work in practice, and at the way that operations of power in our society may shape our desires and behavior, limiting individuals' ability to freely negotiate and give consent.

# NEGOTIATING CONSENT

**Consent Negotiation: The Basics**

Approaching sexual consent from the perspective of bodily autonomy means having respect for your own and your partners' bodily autonomy, treating your partners with the care and consideration due another person, and erring on the side of caution when you are not sure whether they are as into what you are doing as you are. Even from a purely selfish point of view, a bodily autonomy approach makes sense: if we want to be allowed to exercise our own bodily autonomy, we should respect that of others. None of which, of course, means that sex can't be fun, or even that consent negotiation can't be fun. It does, however, mean that sex is not a selfish exercise in using someone else's body for your own gratification—it is a mutual exchange, whether in casual situations or long-term relationships.

So how do we actually agree with another person that we want to have sex, and what kind of sex we want to have?

You may have seen, a few years ago, a viral blog post or video about how sex is a bit like a cup of tea.[1] If you offer someone a cup of tea and they say, "yes please," then go ahead and make that cup of tea; if they're not entirely sure, you can still make them the tea, but don't be offended if they don't drink it; and if they say "no, thank you," or they're asleep, don't force tea down their throat.

This is a great starting point, and in the rest of this chapter we will unpack it a little bit further, considering who exactly should be doing consent negotiation, what we are negotiating, some of the things we can do with consent (such as asking for it, giving it, withholding it, or withdrawing it), as well as some potential complicating factors and frequently asked questions. In many ways, this chapter sets out what consent negotiation would look like in an ideal world, free from power relations and assumptions about what sex is, and where we all have rather fewer hang-ups about expressing our desires or saying no to each other when we feel uncomfortable with something. In chapter 4, we will look at how structural inequalities and other operations of power in society impact consent.

In both sex advice literature and popular culture (the main places where we tend to learn how sex works), the topic of consent is notable primarily for its absence.[2] One of the few places where it does occasionally crop up is in content aimed at teenage audiences. It is almost as if we collectively assume that once we hit 18, we all somehow automatically know how consent works, and we no longer need to discuss it in sex advice materials or popular culture for older audiences.

Yet if the recent global wave of allegations of rape, sexual assault, and sexual harassment against high-profile individuals from all walks of life and the resulting public debate is anything to go by, many (if not most) of us have only a tenuous grasp on ideas of sexual consent. Whether that is because some people have been getting away with abusing their power and violating others' consent for a very long time, because we have very few opportunities to learn about consent and practice it in safe environments, or a mix of both, is a question for another book. Ultimately though, there are too many myths surrounding sex and consent, and learning to negotiate consent is not just for teenagers, but for all of us. Even if this is something you already do as part of your sexual practice, there is always room for reflection and improvement.

As we saw in chapter 2, legal definitions of rape tend to focus on and privilege penile-vaginal intercourse as the sexual act that "counts" in terms of consent. This both reflects and reinforces wider social attitudes about what is and is not sex, and what does and does not require consent. As a result, our discussions and understanding of consent also tend to be disproportionately focused on sexual penetration, and even more narrowly, on penile-vaginal intercourse. From consent education to legal reform campaigns and activist blog posts like the one about the cup of tea, the emphasis tends to be on obtaining consent for penetration.

This idea is in fact so prevalent that even feminist academic researchers sometimes fall into the trap of too narrowly defining what acts exactly require consent. One series of studies, which aimed to establish how US college students negotiated consent, specifically defined the act that was being negotiated as penile-vaginal intercourse. This in turn resulted in a range of other sexual acts such as touching, kissing, and undressing being defined as "consent behaviors"—expressions of consent rather than sexual acts requiring consent in their own right.[3]

But if we approach consent from the point of view of bodily autonomy, the limits of this almost exclusive focus on penetration and penile-vaginal intercourse become clear. While degrees of harm and individual experiences may differ and depend on a range of factors, your bodily autonomy is still violated by being kissed or touched against your will, not only by being penetrated against your will. You have not shown care, respect and consideration for your partner as a person by failing to make sure they were OK with you kissing them, just as you have not shown care by failing to make sure they were OK with you penetrating them. So, the range of acts we need to negotiate consent for is much wider than just penile-vaginal intercourse, or even penetration. If we truly care about our own and our partners' bodily autonomy, we should be ensuring that we and they are consenting to everything we choose to do together, whether that is cuddling, kissing, intercourse, kink, or an orgy.[4]

One of the key implications of this approach to consent is that we have to stop assuming that we know what sex looks like, that there is only one template for how sex goes. You already know the sexual script: you share a few drinks, you kiss, you touch, you undress, a penis goes in a vagina, and the whole thing is over when the cisgender man ejaculates.

We have to open up to a whole range of possibilities normally excluded from this scenario: that the participants may not be exactly one cisgender man and one cisgender woman (they may be trans or non-binary, they may be two cis men or two cis women, there may be more than two of them, in all sorts of gender configurations); that one or more participants may be disabled (visibly or invisibly, in ways that variously impact their experience and expression of sexuality); that we can enjoy and be turned on by a whole range of things not normally part of the standard script (like watching each other masturbate or using sex toys); that, equally, we may not enjoy or be uncomfortable with some or even all of the standard script (it's OK to not like or want penetrative sex); that it's OK for sex not to end in cisgender men orgasming (whether that is because they get bored before they get there, because sexual activities may continue after that, or because the other person withdraws consent for any reason); and that sex does not even necessarily involve more than one person (sometimes learning about bodily autonomy can start and even end with masturbation, and that too is OK).

Rather than sex being a linear process that takes us from A to B, it is a space of possibilities for mutual exploration and enjoyment. Penises don't have to go in vaginas; fingers may go in anuses; mouths and sex toys can be used in all sorts of inventive and exciting ways; your gender or your genital configuration in no way define the roles you can play or the activities you can engage in during sex; sex can be a whole-body experience. Think, then, of consent negotiation as exploring that space. Among the many things you and your partners may each find sexually enjoyable, there may be some overlap, and consent negotiation is about finding that overlap. But it is also important to realize that no overlap may exist, for a whole range of reasons. The person you're into may just not be into you. You may just not share sexual interests. Or they may like you but not want to do any of the things you want to do right now. (Or, of course, vice versa.) In each of those cases, bodily autonomy, consent, and consideration for your partners are paramount, and no means no.

## Key Concepts in Consent Negotiation

Now that we have expanded our idea of what sex is and who can do what, we can start thinking about some of the key concepts in consent negotiation, and how exactly we navigate our way through this space of possibilities with our partners while respecting each other's bodily autonomy.[5]

*Asking* is the first important thing we need to learn to do when it comes to consent. You may have heard people, particularly in the wake of the #MeToo movement, ask if they need to get a legal contract signed every time they have sex. This is an attempt to derail the conversation and minimize the seriousness of sexual violence in everyday situations. In a world free from rape culture, legal contracts have nothing to do with consent, as consent requires communication, care, and respect for your partners as human beings, none of which can easily be regulated by the law.

You can ask for consent in lots of different ways, both verbally and with your body. How exactly you do it will depend on what you are asking a partner to consent to, how well you know that partner, and the specific situation and context. Importantly, asking for consent for sexual acts can (and in many cases should) happen before and outside specifically sexual situations. You can talk about your fantasies over a cup of tea or a glass of wine, or exchange steamy texts. Don't wait until you're all hot and bothered before you check if it's OK to stick a finger up your partner's bum. And whenever you ask, whatever you ask for, make sure your partners know that they can say no. Always listen to the answer and be prepared for that answer to be "no."

Like asking for consent, *giving* consent can be done in many different ways, and will be highly context-dependent. Some psychology research looking into how college students communicate sexual consent indicates that men and women communicate and interpret consent differently. Men tend to initiate sexual contact and practice "removal behaviors" such as moving to a more private space or closing the bedroom door. Women tend to use non-verbal cues such as touching and kissing, as well as passive behaviors such as not telling their partners to stop.[6]

This kind of behaviorist research gives us a picture of how people behave in sexual situations in the messy world we live in, but it struggles to account for *why* we behave in these ways, and it fails to challenge the problematic social structures that these behaviors are both built on and reproduce. And while in some situations this kind of consent communication may be enough, in an ideal world for most of us it probably is not. As well as being highly gendered and heteronormative, it relies on too many assumptions about what sex is, how it works, and who does what. Crucially, it does not take into account two very important factors about consent: first, that consent can be conditional; and second, that for consent to be valid, it has to be continuous.

Saying that consent can be *conditional* means that you can say "yes, I want to do this with you, but only on these conditions." Perhaps the most common examples of conditions attached to consent are those related to safer sex practices. Consent to penetration can be conditional on condom use, consent to oral sex can be conditional on the use of dental dams, and consent to having an open relationship or multiple partners can be conditional on regular STI testing. But there are also other situations where conditional consent applies. For sex workers, for instance, consent is conditional on being paid for their work. (Note also that even if payment is offered, sex workers are free to reject it and withhold their consent. Payment in this case is a necessary but not sufficient condition.)

Conditions we attach to our consent are generally related to our exercise of bodily autonomy. Outside of very specific kink situations, they should not be factors beyond that, such as "I will have sex with you if you do the washing-up," nor the reverse, "If I buy you a drink, you should have sex with me." These would take us back into the territory of the contractual model of consent[7]—the idea that certain unrelated actions by one partner generate an obligation for another partner to engage in sexual activity. While this idea is pervasive in our culture, it is incompatible with the principle of bodily autonomy.

For consent to be valid, it also needs to be continuous. In other words, you are allowed to change your mind about what you are doing at any point during a sexual situation, for any reason, and *withdraw* your consent, and have the right for your bodily autonomy to be respected. It's OK to say to your partner, "Hey, I don't want to do this anymore." You can, if you want, follow this up with, "Let's do something else that's fun for both of us" or you can just ask for the sexual situation to end entirely, and your partner should respect this. Equally, it's OK for your partner to withdraw consent and you should respect this. Your partner's consent withdrawal does not reflect on you as a person or your skills in bed, and may not be about you at all. They may be bored, have a headache, or just not be into the particular activity you are doing. It may not be fun to stop doing something you are really enjoying, but not doing so infringes on others' bodily autonomy and really does reflect on you as a person.

Ensuring your partners' continuous consent does not just mean stop when they say so. If we want to truly respect others' bodily autonomy and share mutually pleasurable sexual experiences with them rather than just using someone else's body for our own gratification, we need to be attuned to both our own and our partners' needs throughout a sexual encounter. This means regularly checking in with them to make sure they are happy, enjoying what you are doing, and continuing to consent.

The final and perhaps most important thing you can do with regards to consent is *withhold* it. You can just say "no," at any time, for any reason whatsoever, and you don't even have to give a reason. Saying "no," however, can be trickier than it sounds. Especially in the kind of rape culture that we live in, where victims of sexual violence are often blamed while those perpetrating it are excused, there are many mixed messages about saying no "properly."

There is a history of rape prevention campaigns aimed at women, teaching them to "just say no" more forcefully, more clearly, or differently. Even in recent high-profile allegations of rape and sexual violence, one of the first responses has frequently been, "Did she say no clearly enough?" Yet research on how we generally decline and refuse things does not back up the idea that women, or victims of sexual violence of any gender, are not expressing themselves clearly enough.[8] Saying no, whether it is to a cup of tea, to going to the pub with friends, or to sex, is a socially tricky act—it is conversationally "dispreferred." We worry about hurting others' feelings and so we tend to soften and couch our "no" in other terms. We tend to give reasons ("I can't go out for a beer tonight, I'm playing football."), thank the person for their offer ("Oh thank you, I would love to, but ..."), or even partially accept ("Not right now, thanks, but maybe later.").

These are commonly accepted, polite ways of refusing offers, regardless what those offers relate to, and most of us understand them as clear refusals, especially outside sexual situations. There is, therefore, no reason why similar ways of doing refusals should be interpreted differently in sexual situations. (Some neuroatypical people, for instance autistic people, report that they struggle with indirect communication like this. There are, however, ways of working around this. You can, for example, talk to your partners before and outside sexual situations about the best ways to communicate with each other.)

There are also reasons why women in heterosexual situations in particular may communicate refusals less directly. Direct communication, and especially a direct refusal, is seen as masculine, and women are frequently socially penalized for unfeminine behaviors. In some situations, women also genuinely fear for their safety if they upset their partner, and therefore will try to soften refusals as much as possible in order to protect themselves. Respect for others' bodily autonomy requires us to listen to our partners and take ambivalence or polite refusals as seriously as an outright "no."

**Consent Negotiation: FAQs**

Discussions of consent frequently prompt a whole host of questions. Some of these can be derailing tactics, such as the seemingly ubiquitous inquiry about legal contracts.

Others are genuine attempts to tease out the details of what is a complex issue. Many are rooted in the fact that we are immersed in rape culture and unlearning that takes conscious effort. Here, then, we will address some of these questions, including, first, a look at the contextual factors that can shape how consent negotiation unfolds and, second, issues around personal boundaries and seduction.

As already hinted above, consent negotiation is highly dependent on context. How you approach it will vary based on how long you have known the person or people involved, whether you have had other sexual encounters with them, how confident you are about being able to openly communicate with them and read them, as well as external factors that may influence your or their ability to meaningfully consent.

Perhaps the most obvious contextual factor in consent negotiation is the nature of your relationship with your partners. Is this a hook-up with a stranger after a night out? Netflix and chill between friends with benefits? A kink party? Or sex with someone you've been together with for years or are married to? These things make a difference, though maybe not always in the ways we expect.

It may be tempting to think that familiarity with partners may make consent negotiation easier, or even provide shortcuts, but that is not a safe assumption to make, as it is based on the misconception that past consent implies future consent. One particularly harmful version of this misconception is the idea that marriage constitutes automatic and perpetual consent. This idea is harmful particularly to women in different-gender marriages and to people in same-gender marriages, as it combines with other ideas—for instance about femininity, masculinity, appropriate gender roles, and what marriage is—to put individuals under significant pressure to consent to sex they may not want.

To some, the idea of automatic consent upon marriage may sound outrageous, or at least outdated, but it took thirty years of campaigning before marital rape was recognized as an offense in England and Wales in 1991,[9] and Germany did not outlaw marital rape until 1997. The fact is that for most of us regardless of jurisdiction, marital rape has been legal for at least part of our lives, and many have internalized the social attitudes that underpin this legal situation. So, for the avoidance of doubt, while in saying "I do" you promise to do quite a lot of things, letting your spouse use your body for their sexual gratification whenever they want to is not one of them. A disparity in sexual desire in long-term relationships is fairly common, but managing it should always involve respect for your partner's bodily autonomy.

It may also be tempting to think that if you have done a particular sexual act with a long-term partner once, or even many times, they will be up for it again. This, too, is a misconception. It may be that they are not in the mood for this particular thing right now, or that they did not enjoy it and never want to do it again. The principle of bodily autonomy continues to apply, and consent negotiation and open communication continue to be vital in marriages and other long-term relationships.

Knowing partners well, however, can have other advantages in consent negotiation. Knowing how your partners communicate, and being able to read their body language as well as their verbal cues, becomes easier over time. If you have established trust, if you are confident that you can say no and it will be respected, and that your partner is comfortable saying no to you—then you have an excellent foundation for day-to-day consent negotiation in a long-term relationship.

On the other extreme, hook-ups and other kinds of sex with people we don't know very well also present their own challenges in consent negotiation. Particularly in a culture that has a very dominant default sexual script centered on penile-vaginal intercourse, there is a lot of pressure to just follow that script, regardless of your own actual desires or those of your partners. Taking a minute to breathe and think about how to go off script with someone you don't know very well can be hard. Yet if we respect our own and others' bodily autonomy, it is vital that we start dismantling that default script in all our sexual interactions, even if that can be awkward or disappointing at times.

The sex educators Meg-John Barker and Justin Hancock suggest approaching potential hook-up situations without the expectation that they will end in sex of any kind.[10] Remembering not only that sex is not a linear path from A to B—that there are other possibilities we can explore together—but also that other kinds of connections and relationships can be valid and pleasurable is a good start. You may have the best sex (in whatever form) of your life, or you may make a new friend, or have a couple of drinks with a stranger and part ways. All of these can be rewarding experiences in their own right, and we need not put ourselves (or others) under pressure to achieve one particular, narrowly defined outcome.

Another common challenge to consent negotiation is impairment to communication and decision-making abilities, for instance through drugs or alcohol. Feminist campaigners have observed with a certain amount of sarcasm that drunkenness is often used to excuse the actions of a person who sexually assaults someone, particularly if he is a man, while at the same time it is used to blame victims, particularly women. Compare and contrast "He was drunk, he didn't know what he was doing" with "She was drunk, what did she think would happen?" Rape prevention campaigns have long told women not to get drunk, or warned them to watch drinks being made (thus guaranteeing they have not been spiked). Yet the equivalent campaigns telling men not to spike drinks and not to have sex with

You may have the best sex (in whatever form) of your life, or you may make a new friend, or have a couple of drinks with a stranger and part ways. All of these can be rewarding experiences in their own right, and we need not put ourselves (or others) under pressure to achieve one particular, narrowly defined outcome.

someone while drunk to avoid potentially misinterpreting consent communication do not seem to exist outside of parodies in online feminist circles.

If someone is clearly too out of it to consent, then helping that person find a safe place to sleep it off or recover is your best bet, but in less extreme situations there are no hard and fast rules on drugs or alcohol and consent. Noting and challenging the double standards in heterosexual relationships and hook-ups, however, is a good starting point. Keeping the principle of bodily autonomy in mind can also help here: knowing yourself and your own response to alcohol or drugs, asking yourself whether you are in a position to respect another person's boundaries when you are under the influence.

It is also worth remembering that different communities have different standards when it comes to drugs and alcohol. Many kink and BDSM practitioners strongly advise against consuming *any* drugs or alcohol prior to or during a scene. This is partly because some BDSM activities (a variety of eroticism or roleplaying including bondage and discipline, submission and dominance, or sadomasochism) can be genuinely dangerous, leading to serious injury or even death if practiced carelessly. Partly, however, these attitudes are also rooted in a concern for informed consent and a desire to ensure all parties are fully present and able to communicate, to ask for, give, receive, withhold or withdraw consent at any point.

Other communities have a long history of drug use and sex. Practices such as Party and Play (P&P) or chemsex, which involve using specific drugs to enhance sexual pleasure and are common among some gay and bisexual men in urban areas, have gained mainstream media attention in recent years, partly because of their association with several high-profile murder cases. This has led to a spate of "something must be done" articles (including an editorial in the *British Medical Journal*) and statements from the UK government in particular. Yet many commentators tend to ignore the social and historical context of these practices, which are rooted in the oppression and marginalization of queer communities throughout the twentieth century, the emergence and subsequent closure of a range of gay social venues between the 1990s and 2000s, the emergence of hook-up apps such as Grindr, and the development of technologies and cultures around psychoactive drugs.

There is limited academic research on chemsex and related practices, but what there is tends to indicate that chemsex is deeply tied to the issues of marginalization and pressures to assimilate that face contemporary queer cultures, as well as to questions of masculinity and a search for intimacy. Key concerns expressed around chemsex tend to focus on sexual health and particularly HIV and hepatitis C transmission; issues of consent have emerged only more recently, primarily driven by community charities rather than academic researchers or public health practitioners.

Ultimately the principle of bodily autonomy remains valid, even in environments where drug use prior to and during sex is normalized: you continue to have the right to withhold or withdraw your consent, you continue to have an obligation to respect other people's consent decisions.[11]

Drugs and alcohol are not the only factors that may impair communication. In an increasingly globalized world it is easy to assume that we all share the same cultural references and underpinnings, but partners from different cultural backgrounds may well find themselves struggling with culture shock in both their day-to-day relationship and when it comes to sex and consent. Our upbringing and cultural background has a significant impact on how we think about sex. The languages we speak give us access to different ways of thinking about it. And the default scripts we fall back on may be different. Consciously unpacking the assumptions you are making about sex—whether in a casual hook-up or in a long-term relationship—takes work but can help bridge some of these communication gaps.

Another question commonly raised in discussions of consent concerns the place of seduction in a culture that places value on consent. It is worth briefly examining seduction as a concept, as it can tell us quite a bit about how we think about issues of consent and interpersonal relationships. Seduction, in the way it is used in these conversations, generally implies persuading someone to have sex with you when that person has expressed unwillingness to do so. A host of cultural tropes here play on a constructed disconnect between mind and body, between what is socially appropriate and what we may desire.

Like our dominant sexual scripts, these tropes are highly gendered and heteronormative. They are built on ideas of how men and women *should* feel and act when it comes to sex. They assume men who are active initiators of sex, and women who are passive gatekeepers, frequently less driven by their own sexual desire than by considerations of social standing. These tropes are inextricably intertwined with the "token resistance to sex" myth: the idea that women will refuse sex even if they secretly want it, for a range of possible reasons. The concept of seduction, then, is premised on the notion that "no" does not always mean "no," that women in particular cannot be trusted to clearly communicate their consent or nonconsent, and that it is acceptable to push boundaries until "no" becomes "yes."

Boundaries are a useful concept when thinking about what seduction actually means and how it relates to consent. Boundaries are the line between what is and is not OK for us. They can relate to sexual situations, but also to a variety of other things, such as social situations and casual interactions with others. Preferring to be addressed by a nickname rather than your full name may be a boundary. Being comfortable in small groups but not in large gatherings may be a boundary. Not liking certain foods or preferring handshakes over hugs are also examples of non-sexual boundaries we may set for ourselves. Similarly, in sexual situations, we may be comfortable with some kinds of touch or sexual acts but not others, or we may not want sex right now or with a particular person at all.

Knowing where our boundaries are, both in sexual and non-sexual situations, can sometimes be tricky. It can take time to work out what we like, what we don't like, and where the line is. Communicating our boundaries to others can also be a balancing act between exercising our autonomy and respecting social conventions. We frequently have to rely on others to ask us where our boundaries are, but they may not be in the habit of doing so. If you go to a dinner party and your host has not checked what foods you do and do not like, for instance, do you discreetly pick the mushrooms out of your dish, only eat the parts of the meal you can, or possibly even risk an allergic reaction? Communication of boundaries is very much a two-way process, and can break down completely if one party does not do their part.

A big issue when it comes to consent and boundaries is that those who have no interest in respecting our boundaries can exploit the social awkwardness we feel in communicating them. Many of the more aggressive sales techniques involve exactly that kind of exploitation: putting someone in a position where saying no would be seen as impolite, or even cause a scene, in order to push them toward saying yes. We can also see this in social interactions—for instance, when someone demands to be greeted with a hug or cheek kisses and relies on the other person's reluctance to be openly confrontational. Questioning others' stated boundaries, demanding justifications for them, or nagging them once they have expressed a boundary are also behaviors that exploit social conventions in order to push or outright ignore those boundaries.

Seduction attempts more often than not are attempts to push boundaries, stated or implied. People sometimes do give in to them, but frequently that is not out of genuine desire but out of fear of worse consequences. In reality, even if "no" does become "yes," it does so under pressure and coercion, and rarely in a way that is respectful of someone's bodily autonomy.

## Technology to the Rescue?

In the wake of the #MeToo campaign, there has been a renewed focus on addressing sexual violence in a range of ways. Mobile phone apps are one recent development ostensibly designed to improve consent negotiation and provide a clear record of consent. These apps claim to do several things: provide a way to communicate boundaries, clearly record explicit consent or help you communicate non-consent, and, depending on the app, help you re-cord a violation and pursue it through the courts as a civil case based on contract law. From a feminist point of view grounded in respect for bodily autonomy, it should become clear fairly quickly why this approach is highly problematic.

While providing prompts for individuals to discuss what they may or may not like and consent to may be a good start, at least one of the apps currently on the mar-ket treats boundaries not as a discussion but rather as an automated checklist, framing this as a way of removing the awkwardness of communicating about consent. Yet while talking about our sexual desires and boundaries can be difficult and awkward, what is removed here is not the awkwardness but the actual communication. Nuance, emotion, and humanity are lost in toggle switches labeled, for instance, "condom use" and "BDSM."

Another app allows the user to play a video of a policeman forcefully saying no, with the developers claim-ing that showing this video to someone pressuring you for sex makes your refusal clearer. This too is problematic, as it is grounded in rape culture myths about unclear com-munication and token resistance. Ultimately, we should not need videos of policemen telling us "no" to respect our partners' bodily autonomy.

Rather than having these apps become a factor in the protection of potential victims, a concern arises here that

Ultimately, we should not need videos of policemen telling us "no" to respect our partners' bodily autonomy.

perpetrators of sexual violence will use them to "prove" consent was given, as the electronic record of consent may be seen as overriding any subsequent verbal communication. App developers have sought to reassure users in their marketing materials that consent can be revoked verbally at any time, but for that to be true there would have to be a widespread cultural and legal acceptance of the idea of consent withdrawal as legitimate. This is currently not the case, as rape myths, such as the token resistance to sex myth, are still both culturally pervasive and extensively leveraged by defense lawyers in the criminal justice system. The framing of sex as a contractual transaction that consent apps encourage is not conducive to open and honest communication, to listening and checking in with partners, or to feeling confident that consent withdrawal would be respected.

It may be tempting to see apps like these as a pragmatic stopgap while we work on the wider project of dismantling rape culture, but they are highly likely to cause more harm than good. They actively reproduce the dominant attitudes and assumptions of rape culture, dominant sexual scripts and gender roles, and myths about how we communicate about sex. They are not likely to actually prevent sexual assault, as in one case consent withdrawal relies on having access to your phone and in another it remains as difficult to prove in a court of law as it is without using the app. And while in a very limited number of cases they may provide recourse to justice either through recording evidence of an assault or through contract law, they are unlikely to actually address the structural issues the criminal justice system has with dealing with sexual violence.

Consent negotiation, then, remains a messy, sometimes awkward activity between human beings, not a legal or contractual matter. Guided by a respect for bodily autonomy, our challenge is to dismantle the dominant sexual script that tells us that sex has to take one particular form, to ensure we are asking for consent not just to penetration but to other sexual activities too, that we are prepared to hear the answer, and that we continue to check in with our partners and make sure their consent is continuous. And that is only the beginning. In the next chapter, we will explore how social structures and inequalities of power shape our thinking and behavior when it comes to sex and consent, and what we can do about it.

# SEX AND POWER— BETWEEN YES AND NO

**Unwanted Sex**

The practicalities of negotiating consent can at times be tricky, as we saw in chapter 3. This is true even in the best of circumstances: when everyone involved is genuinely into what we are doing, when we want to respect someone else's bodily autonomy, when we know how our partners communicate, when we are happy to communicate our own desires and boundaries and feel confident that our partners will respect them. But are there other external factors that might influence the choices we make with regard to consent? How do the ways in which we are taught to think about what sex is and how it works affect what we choose to do, how, when, and with whom? Are some choices easier to make than others? Are "yes" and "no" equally available options, or are there forces and operations of power in our society that might nudge us one way rather than the other?

One very common experience that begins to shed a light on some of these questions is "unwanted sex": sometimes individuals will consent (in a legal sense) to having sex even if they do not want it. Sometimes they will even initiate it. Sometimes, we may choose to have sex for reasons other than desire (for instance as work, or as a way of becoming pregnant). But in many cases unwanted sex is experienced as a violation, or at least as something not quite right, and nonetheless consented to.

Unwanted sex is well documented both in casual situations (hook-ups, friends with benefits arrangements, etc.) and in long-term relationships.[1] Most of the available research focuses on women and unwanted sex, but there is an increasing amount of anecdotal evidence that men and non-binary people experience this too. The reported prevalence of unwanted sex begins to raise questions about the limits of bodily autonomy. Why do we consent to sex we do not want? What other factors might influence our decision making?

In long-term relationships, unwanted sex is sometimes explained as relationship maintenance: doing things for your partner, even if you do not necessarily want to, in order to make or keep them happy or because they also do similar things for you. Women who experience unwanted sex in casual situations report that their self-image and

Are "yes" and "no" equally available options, or are there forces and operations of power in our society that might nudge us one way rather than the other?

ideas about what it means to be a sexually enlightened woman in our society are implicated in their experiences. Similarly, men who speak of unwanted sex report that they feel under pressure from societal expectations to be sexually active and to always want sex. Sexual orientation and relationship type also play a role in these experiences. Women in relationships with women, for instance, may make a conscious effort to ensure a certain amount or frequency of sex in their relationship, as they feel the romantic and sexual nature of the relationship would be invalidated otherwise, making it indistinguishable from a friendship.

All of these experiences point toward an important way in which power is exercised and individual agency and autonomy are limited in our society. The French philosopher Michel Foucault argues that power operates through discourse—the way we talk about things shapes how we see the world and even how we behave.[2] There is a long tradition in Western philosophy that regards individuals as unified subjects: coherent, rational, autonomous, whole selves in possession of agency. More recently, feminist theorists as well as philosophers working in the postmodern tradition, such as Foucault, have called this view into question. Alternative views have been proposed according to which subjects are fragmented and contradictory, shaped by their social environment, and *constructed* through discourse.[3]

Feminist theorists have built on Foucault's ideas to show how, for instance, beauty standards in our society generate practices such as dieting and exercise, which have a direct impact on women's bodies.[4] Others have argued that the ways we think about sex, sexuality, and gender roles—the discourses about these things that are dominant in our society—produce a vast grey area of sexual behaviors and encounters that lie on a spectrum between mutually consensual sex and rape.

The ways we see ourselves or want others to see us, the resources we have access to in naming our experiences and desires (or lack thereof), the dominant ideas about what counts as sex, who should be having sex, and what sex means in our society all work in subtle ways to make some choices easier than others.[5] In this way, the operation of power doesn't only stop us from doing certain things. Rather, it is *productive*: it constructs and produces subjects, bodies, and practices. It also operates multi-directionally rather than top-down. It is not exercised by the state, but by each of us over each other and ourselves, in a multitude of competing and contradictory ways.

In the remainder of this chapter we will return to some of the above examples in more detail to explore how the operation of power through discourse—that is, the dominant ideas about gender, sex, and sexuality in our society—may produce subjects who take some courses of action over others, and how those discourses *shape* our exercise of agency and bodily autonomy with regard to sex and consent.

## The Dominant Discourses of (Hetero)Sex

If the way we talk about things shapes how we view the world and how we behave, the way we talk about gender and sex is likely to have a significant impact on how we think about consent, and on our sexual practice. Investigating such dominant ideas of heterosexual sex and relationships involving a man and a woman, the feminist psychologist Wendy Hollway has identified three key discourses that shape our views of sex and of gender roles in sex: the male sexual drive discourse, the have/hold discourse, and the permissive discourse.[6] Although their heteronormativity limits their analytical usefulness at times, these three dominant ideas highlight how the operation of power through discourse may shape our behavior and go some way toward explaining why some individuals may choose to consent to unwanted sex. They also show how this operation of power is distinctly *gendered*, that is, it has different effects particularly on men and women.

### The Male Sexual Drive Discourse
The male sexual drive discourse tells us that sex (specifically partnered, heterosexual sex) is a biological necessity for

men. It casts men as less in control of their sexual desires and arousal than women. In this way it at least partially absolves men of responsibility for their actions when aroused. As feminist campaigners have pointed out, we can see the operation of the male sexual drive discourse in cultural practices that compel women to dress a certain way to avoid provoking male desire. School dress codes, for example, require girls to cover up so as not to distract boys, whose reactions to certain types of clothing are deemed natural and appropriately male. Such rules excuse boys' behavior—their distraction and even the harassment of girls—and instead transfer the blame for it to girls. Common rape myths and victim-blaming perceptions, such as the idea that women provoke their attackers through the way they dress or act, are also an extension of the male sexual drive discourse.

We can see, then, that the male sexual drive discourse is directly harmful to women in that it constructs them as responsible for men's behavior, and as a result blames them for consent violations committed by men. But it can also be harmful to men. Because this discourse constructs men as constantly seeking heterosexual sex, it generates the expectation that sex is the main type of interpersonal interaction that men seek with people they are even only potentially attracted to, and that they are constantly up for it.

There is no room here for friendship or working relationships. There is also little room in the male sexual drive discourse for emotional bonds beyond the sexual. Ideas of what it means to be a man are deeply intertwined with this discourse, with men's self-worth all too often being measured by the number of their sexual conquests and their emotional unavailability. Some men report feeling pressured by these constructions of masculinity and ideas of the male sexual drive to always consent to, or even initiate sex, even if they do not want it or would prefer a different kind of bond and experience.

### The "Have/Hold" Discourse

Another dominant idea about heterosexual sex and relationships that shapes the way individuals act in relation to sex is the "have/hold" discourse. Named after the traditional phrasing of Christian marriage vows ("to have and to hold") originating in the *Book of Common Prayer*, this is the idea that women, while less interested in sex than men, have a strong interest in long-term, stable, romantic relationships. This also casts sex as something that should only or predominantly take place within such relationships, and puts the responsibility for ensuring this on women. Women who fail to do this, for instance by having casual sex, suffer social consequences. They are stigmatized and shamed as "sluts." If they experience sexual violence, they are constructed as having brought it onto themselves through their immoral and unfeminine behavior. This is true both socially and in legal practice, where a rape victim's sexual history may be used as a reason to not prosecute a case or in some jurisdictions brought up in court to undermine her credibility.

The male sexual drive and the have/hold discourses have their origins partly in Christian approaches to gender roles and sexuality. Extreme versions of these discourses have been (re)elevated to religious doctrine and enshrined in religious institutions in US evangelical communities. This in turn has had the effect of enabling systemic sexual abuse within these communities, something that is only just emerging, for instance under the #ChurchToo hashtag on social media. A look at how exactly these discourses are leveraged and taken to extreme in evangelical communities can shed some light on their operation in wider society and rape culture.

Evangelical doctrine fully subscribes to the idea of the male sexual drive (or "lust") as uncontrollable and insatiable. It also subscribes to the idea of women as less or not at all interested in sex, thereby casting them as the gatekeepers to sex. Sex outside of marriage is constructed as impure and sinful, and responsibility for it is placed squarely on the shoulders of women. At the same time, women in evangelical communities are taught to be subservient to men from a young age and are barred from leadership posts within churches. Institutionally and doctrinally, this is an abuser's dream, as has become clear from the countless stories emerging from a growing "exvangelical" movement. Abuse in evangelical churches appears to permeate all levels, from youth group leaders to superstar preachers in megachurches.

One common element in many victims' accounts reveals how these churches' doctrinal teachings not only enabled the abuse by putting abusive men in positions of authority but also systematically deflected the blame onto the victims. Women fully believed that they had failed in their task as gatekeepers to sex, that it was them who had sinned. In some cases, abusers took advantage of this, shaming their victims further and thereby ensuring that they could not seek support. Where victims did seek support within church structures, institutions protected abusers, blamed victims, and in some cases even told victims that the solution would be to marry their abusers.

In evangelical communities, the extreme application of the male sexual drive and have/hold discourses, combined with other doctrinal and institutional factors, has allowed rape culture to fester. Women's self-worth in particular is tied to a toxic cocktail of sexual purity and submission to men, putting them in an impossible double bind. But it is important to understand that these are not isolated communities, and that their thinking is highly influential both in and beyond the United States. "Purity culture" has for several decades been exported beyond evangelical communities and used as a recruitment tool by churches. Evangelical organizations have developed and continue to deliver "abstinence only" sex education (frequently the only kind of sex education available) in schools across the United States, reproducing extreme versions of the male sexual drive and have/hold discourses, and fostering rape-supportive attitudes among young people.[7] More diluted versions of these discourses then operate throughout society with similar though perhaps more subtle effects.

### The Permissive Discourse

A third, more recently developed idea about gender and sexuality that operates alongside the male sexual drive and have/hold discourses is the permissive discourse. It originates in ideas about free love and sexual expression of the 1960s. Like the male sexual drive discourse, the permissive discourse sees sex and sexuality as natural, biological. At first glance, ideas about free love are less gendered than either the male sexual drive or the have/hold discourse. Rather, they construct sexual expression as a right regardless of gender. They encourage us to explore and express our sexuality, which on the surface may seem harmless and even benign. But in its interaction with other dominant ideas, the permissive discourse may be just as powerful and potentially harmful in the way it shapes our choices.

The permissive discourse frequently combines with some more recent ideas about sexual liberation and personal responsibility to put pressure on women to engage in sometimes unwanted casual sex. Since the 1980s we have seen the rise of neoliberal ideas, which place emphasis on (and measure human value in terms of) individualism, agency, and personal responsibility. The ideal neoliberal subject is constructed as entrepreneurial, constantly seeking self-improvement in all areas of life. They are presented as freely choosing actions from an almost unlimited range of options and bearing full responsibility for those choices, regardless of structural or social constraints.

Think, for instance, of how we tend to talk about stress, mental health, and work–life balance in the workplace. We tend to tell people to look after themselves: go for a walk, do exercise, don't work late, eat well. In this neoliberal view, we are all responsible for managing our own mental health and work–life balance. The hidden assumption is that we can choose to perform actions that make us better at this, and conversely that if we are still experiencing problems, that is our own fault for making the wrong choices. What this model neglects is the role of structural factors beyond our control: we may not be able to cut down our hours because our pay or performance review depend on them; we may not be able to exercise because we are working two jobs to make ends meet; we may not be able to eat well because of time or financial constraints. Neoliberal ideas actively work to obscure the role of exploitative or oppressive structures by shifting responsibility to the individual.

Neoliberal ideas operate similarly when it comes to sexual consent. If a good neoliberal subject should always seek self-improvement, and if, as the permissive discourse would have us believe, the expression and exploration of sexuality is a key part of that improvement project, then there is significant pressure to engage in sex in order to continually improve ourselves. And if we freely chose those actions (because social factors and structural pressures are disregarded), then we must also bear the responsibility for them. So, if we consensually engage in sex we do not want due to the social pressures of the permissive discourse and dominant ideas about self-improvement, then we have no one else to blame but ourselves.

Young women who experience unwanted but consensual sex frequently use the permissive discourse combined with their understanding of themselves as sexually liberated and always in search of self-improvement to explain those experiences and take responsibility for them. One participant in a study on unwanted sex even referred to her multiple experiences of unwanted sex as "wonderful" because she felt they had all taught her something.[8] Here, dominant ideas about sexual expression and personal responsibility limit individuals' ability to say no to sex they do not want, and deflect the blame for these experiences back onto the individual.

## Dominant Discourses, Contradictory Pressures

Dominant discourses like these may evolve over time, and they rarely do so coherently. This is evident from the fact that all three of these discourses are operational in our society, yet they are also all contradictory. The have/hold and male sexual drive discourses reflect much older ideas about sexuality than the permissive discourse. They may also not be equally dominant across different sections of society, but they are still pervasive. The contradictions of the three discourses put contradictory pressures particularly on women, who are constructed as responsible for either not provoking or satisfying men's sexual needs, as gatekeepers to sex who are to ensure that it only happens under the right circumstances, and as responsible for expressing their own sexuality. The three discourses also set up men and women in opposition to each other, stigmatizing women who fail to balance the contradictory demands put on them while also leaving little room for men to explore intimacy and emotional connection beyond sex.

The three discourses are a good starting point in understanding the contradictory pressures society puts on us when it comes to sex, particularly as they relate to gender roles. A useful next step is examining how sex itself is discursively constructed. What are the dominant discourses that structure what counts as sex, who does what, and how it all works?

## Sexual Scripts

A good way to think about how we define what sex is and how it works is as a kind of script. We already began to explore in chapter 2 how sexual scripts are another way in which power operates in our society to shape how we think and act in relation to sex. Viewing sexuality through a script theory lens allows us to examine more closely some of the assumptions we make about how sex *should* work, as well as account for at least some of the ways in which individual agency and autonomy are shaped by the discursive construction of sex and sexuality.

Sexual script theory originates in the symbolic interactionism movement within sociology and was first developed in the 1970s.[9] It is a reaction against two conceptions of sex that were dominant at the time and are still highly influential today. The first is the idea that sex and human sexuality can be explained purely as a biological instinct. This idea is reflected in the male sexual drive discourse, which sees men as biologically driven to seek heterosexual sex. It is also present, albeit more obliquely, in evolutionary psychology variants of the have/hold discourse, which seek to explain women's alleged preference for long-term stable relationships through evolutionary factors.

Sexual script theory also reacted to a second idea regarding sex: the psychoanalytic approach, rooted in Freudian ideas of sexual drives and their interaction with the demands and restrictions society puts on us. At its core, psychoanalysis too sees sex as biological, but it casts it in conflict with the social dimension of our experiences.

In contrast to both of these, a sociological approach to sex sees it not as entirely or even mainly biological but as a social phenomenon. The way we *do* sex is profoundly shaped by our social structures and the ideas we have about it. What counts as sex, who does what, and how, can vary widely across historical periods and cultures, indicating that our sexual practices—at least a significant component of them—are indeed culturally and socially constructed: they are produced by discourse. Sexual scripts then are the culturally dominant ideas about how sex *should* work: what counts as sex (or even what counts as erotic!), who does what, under what circumstances, in what order. Without access to the appropriate scripts, according to script theory, we might find ourselves in a situation that has all the components of a sexual situation (for instance, privacy, a partner we might be attracted to, nudity, etc.), and not perceive it as a sexual situation at all.

Western cultures in the early twenty-first century have certain dominant sexual scripts. These scripts are highly gendered, as well as cis- and heteronormative. We tend to define sex as penile-vaginal intercourse that happens between one cisgender man and one cisgender woman. Men are seen as the active initiators of sex, women as passive gatekeepers. We tend to place the starting point of sex somewhere around kissing and touching, and the endpoint at a cisgender man's ejaculation, and there is a clear line of progression between these two points. There is some latitude in the script for things like safer sex practices and types of relationship, but by and large this is how we think of sex in our culture.

Thinking ourselves outside of this dominant paradigm takes conscious effort, and doing so in the context of partnered sex is particularly difficult. This is one way in which the existence of dominant scripts shapes our desires and our actions when it comes to sex. If you are fully immersed in the dominant script and that is your only conception of sex, even just imagining something else is an almost insurmountable obstacle. If, for instance, you are a survivor of sexual violence and parts of this script are traumatic and triggering for you but you have no access to alternatives, your choice may be as limited as not engaging in partnered sex at all, or doing so in ways that are harmful to you.

Even if we have done the work of thinking through and finding alternative scripts that are more appealing to us, we are still operating in a culture that has one particular, dominant idea of how sex works. So, finding potential partners who either already have or are willing to reconsider the dominant sexual script themselves is a challenge and puts practical limits on our options for exercising agency and autonomy in consent negotiation.

Sexual scripts can also interact with other dominant discourses to affect how we think about sex, relationships, and consent. One example of this is the strong association between sexual and romantic relationships in our culture, which itself is a reflection of the have/hold discourse. And while this association has been destabilized since the 1960s through, for instance, the permissive discourse, this destabilization has largely been one-directional. So a sexual relationship can but does not have to be romantic (think, for instance, of hook-ups and friends-with-benefits arrangements). But a romantic relationship is generally seen as necessarily also sexual. Only with the advent of asexual activism in the last decade or so have we seen attempts to destabilize the link between the two in this direction.

The construction of romantic relationships as necessarily sexual puts pressure on individuals to engage in potentially unwanted sex to maintain a long-term romantic relationship. Think of the huge amount of sex advice literature on how to keep the "spark" alive in your marriage: they reflect this construction. Many people report that over time in a long-term relationship they lose interest in sex (sometimes as a result of a change in circumstances such as the arrival of children). Some of them are perfectly happy with this, yet they find themselves under significant pressure to maintain a sexual relationship, and then they find themselves engaging in unwanted sex as a kind of relationship-maintenance practice.

How we conceptualize what is and is not romantic in the context of dominant sexual scripts may also affect whether and how we can negotiate consent and exercise our bodily autonomy. As our sexual relationships move from casual to more committed and romantic, we tend to change our sexual practices, particularly concerning sexual health. This is driven by the assumption that a committed romantic relationship is also sexually exclusive, and as a result the focus of sexual health practices shifts from protection from STIs to pregnancy prevention. Cisgender women in relationships with men then frequently find themselves under significant pressure to dispense with condoms and other barrier methods and move to hormonal contraception instead.[10] This in turn can have a range of negative effects on women, including not only the sometimes significant side effects of hormonal contraception but also potential exposure to STIs.

Dominant sexual scripts are particularly harmful to those they marginalize or exclude. Queer people are one such group. As the dominant sexual script is built on the assumption of cisgender partners of different genders and prescribes strict roles and sequences of events, lesbian, gay, bisexual, transgender, intersex, asexual, aromantic, and other people who don't fit into the allosexual, cis and straight framework do not find themselves reflected in it. This has some interesting and at times contradictory effects. On the one hand, the absence of a dominant script to follow leaves a space for exploration and open communication: you and your partner have to make your own script. On the other hand, the dominant script may still nudge individuals down specific paths, or harm them in other ways.

Disabled people are also frequently excluded from dominant sexual scripts in two ways. They are commonly desexualized, in the sense that we tend to think of disabled people as not having sexual needs, experiencing sexual attraction, or having sex. Some disabled people may very well be asexual, but the two are not necessarily correlated: many disabled people do in fact experience sexual attraction and have sex. But dominant sexual scripts exclude many disabled people whose disabilities mean that they cannot engage in the kind of sex sanctioned by the script. As a result, some disabled people find themselves stepping outside the script, rewriting it in ways that work for them in their own intimate relationships, or finding wider communities where alternative expressions of sexuality are encouraged and supported.[11]

We can see from accounts of people excluded from dominant sexual scripts that those scripts are far from universal in their application. For some there is no script to follow at all, while for others the dominant script just does not fit very well. In fact, sexual script theory accounts for this by suggesting that scripts exist at three different levels. The dominant script we have been discussing so far exists at the cultural level. But we also have scripts at the individual level (the things we personally find sexy, the ways we would like to engage in sex), and the interpersonal level (the mash-up of cultural and individual scripts we ultimately end up negotiating with partners). Significant disjunctures between scripts at different levels may exist even for individuals who otherwise fit the nondisabled, cisgender, allo- and heterosexual "norm" that cultural scripts assume.

Negotiating and resolving these disjunctures is key if we are to exercise agency and bodily autonomy and if our consent is to be meaningful. Researchers have identified three key strategies that individuals tend to use to resolve disjunctures between sexual scripts at different levels.[12] Some of them are more successful in enabling individuals to exercise bodily autonomy and helping them challenge dominant discursive constructions than others. The first such strategy is conformity: you go along with the dominant cultural script even if ultimately it doesn't work for you. Consenting to unwanted sex is frequently an example of conformity, as is following the default, penile-vaginal intercourse script even when there are other sexual activities you would prefer. Here, the existence of the dominant script constructs one particular way to have sex as the obvious and default choice and shapes individuals' desires and actions.

There are other ways to reconcile disjunctures between sexual scripts at the cultural, individual, and interpersonal levels. A second key strategy is exception finding. People who employ this strategy broadly subscribe to the dominant cultural script while also finding ways in which it does not apply to them or their relationships. You may, for instance, think that your own relationship is different from the norm, that the way you and your partner do gender roles is non-conforming, or engage in "off-script" sexual practices. Even if you are not fundamentally challenging the cultural script, this kind of exception finding can be an effective way to exercise agency and autonomy.

The final strategy here is to seek to transform the dominant sexual script at the cultural level. This involves not just finding exceptions in your private life and sexual practice, but questioning and seeking to destabilize dominant scripts. This can be done, for instance, by seeking out like-minded communities, engaging in conversation about the assumptions that underlie default scripts and common sexual practices, and continually developing your own understanding. Feminist, asexual, queer, disabled, and some BDSM communities have mounted a series of successful challenges and destabilized dominant sexual scripts and gender roles. They have done this both in limited localized ways and in ways that have had a wider lasting impact, enabling others to challenge the operation of power through dominant discourses and sexual scripts in their own lives and potentially making alternative choices, desires, and practices more obvious or easier to access.

Disjunctures in sexual scripts and the strategies we use to negotiate them are a key mechanism for long-term change in dominant sexual scripts. Individuals may employ different strategies with different partners, or at different times in their lives. They may find ways to challenge the operation of the default script in their own private lives, and that may be enough for them, opening up a space for creativity, bodily autonomy, and meaningful consent within the wider constraints of social structures and dominant discourses. Or they may seek to effect wider cultural change. We have seen examples of such change, for instance, in the at least partial incorporation of safer sex practices in the cultural sexual script particularly in the wake of the HIV epidemic of the 1980s and 1990s. We may be seeing a further shift regarding consent right now, in the wake of the #MeToo movement. We will explore what effective, lasting change may look like in chapter 7.

## Identity, Marginalization, and Consent

As we have seen in the operation of the male sexual drive and permissive discourses, and the respective interaction of each with ideas of masculinity and the neoliberal subject, one of the key ways in which power operates through discourse is by *constructing subjects*. This means that how we talk about people or groups of people, how we as a society treat them, shapes who they are, makes some choices easier to access than others, and thereby shapes their actions when it comes to sex.

Sometimes these effects are very obviously material. We can see this, for instance, in the recent controversy over transgender people's use of public bathrooms appropriate to their gender. The way transgender people are talked about—misgendered, and their identity denied— has a significant material impact on their lives, and exposes them to the risk of violence and harm.

At other times, the way the discursive construction of subjects operates to oppress and shape individual agency can be more insidious. This is frequently the case when it comes to issues of sexual consent. We have already touched on the way the male sexual drive discourse creates an expectation for men to always seek sex while making it more difficult for them to seek other types of intimate connections. The way society constructs us as subjects, and the ways in which we as a result view ourselves, can have an impact on the choices that are available to us and thereby on the choices we make.

These effects can also be compounded if we experience multiple marginalizations. For instance, the ways in which we are constructed as women may intersect with the ways in which we are constructed as black, or queer, or disabled to put particular pressures on us and shape our experiences in particular ways.[13] In the remainder of this chapter, we will look at some examples of how the discursive construction of some marginalized subjects can shape their choices and actions when it comes to sex and consent.

One very common discourse about what is "normal" and "human" posits that experiencing sexual attraction to other people is part of what makes us human. Thinking back to the three discourses of (hetero)sexuality we explored at the beginning of this chapter, both the male sexual drive discourse and the permissive discourse are predicated on the assumption that sex and sexual attraction are natural, biological, and part of the normal human experience. Yet not everyone experiences sexual attraction, and not everyone who does, does so in the same way. People who do not experience sexual attraction in the same way as the majority are frequently pathologized. There is a pervasive idea that something must be wrong with them, and that it can be fixed, for instance through therapy or meeting the right person.

Over the last ten or fifteen years, asexuality and other related concepts, such as demisexuality and aromanticism, have emerged as distinct identities under the queer umbrella. This development has largely been driven by activists, the formation of an asexual community in online spaces,[14] and to an extent by scholars who have researched asexuality. Asexual activism has highlighted a number of ways in which the presumption that everyone is allosexual (i.e., experiences sexual attraction), harms asexual people and limits their exercise of bodily autonomy.

One example of this is the complete lack of coverage of asexual identities and experiences in both sex and relationships education and (perhaps more crucially) mainstream popular culture. This means that unless an asexual person is lucky enough to stumble upon online asexual communities, they may not have access to the language and ideas to describe who they are or to make sense of their experiences. Combined with a general expectation that everyone is allosexual and should at some point have sex because it is natural, this puts asexual people in a position where they may consent to sex they do not want simply because it is the done thing. One asexual commentator on Twitter described early sexual experiences, consented to before coming to identify as asexual, "like being raped by no one in particular."[15]

Asexual activists and scholars researching asexuality have coined the term "compulsory sexuality" to describe the discourses and systems at work here.[16] Compulsory sexuality describes a collection of discourses, ideas and practices. These include the idea that sexual attraction is natural and something that all humans experience, that it is necessary in order to live a full life and relate to others in appropriate ways, and that sexual and romantic attraction (as well as a variety of other kinds of attraction) necessarily go together. Articulating the idea of compulsory sexuality in turn has allowed asexual activists to disentangle some of the assumptions involved in it and develop concepts such as different types of attraction (sexual, romantic, aesthetic, etc.) that may but do not have to be correlated. It has also enabled people under the broad asexual and aromantic umbrella to push back against societal pressures and to better exercise their own agency when it comes to sex and consent.[17]

The idea of compulsory sexuality as a mechanism through which power operates is useful not just when considering asexuality. It helps highlight a range of other intersectional effects regarding consent on different groups of people and different kinds of bodies. The association between allosexuality and "normality" or "humanity" means that a discourse of desexualization can be used as a means of social control against marginalized groups. By constructing some groups as non-sexual, they are declared deviant, other, or something less than human. There is a wealth of research that has shown how this discourse is leveraged, for instance against older and disabled people, Asian men, and fat people.[18]

Discursive desexualization in turn can shape the choices available to those it is leveraged against in their day-to-day lives and sexual practice. Because desexualization

is closely related to dehumanization and othering, someone who experiences it may feel a need to react against
it by "proving" their own sexuality. There is also significant cultural pressure on individuals to do so. Think, for
instance, of the popular cultural trope of the fat girl in
high school who suddenly receives sexual and romantic
attention from a boy. The expectation of her is that she
is grateful for that attention and consents to whatever he
demands in an attempt to counteract her own desexualization and dehumanization. This trope carries over into
the real world, and fat women are very much expected to
be grateful for any attention they receive and not to reject
potential partners.

Desexualization also affects women in relationships
with women, as women's sexuality tends to be discounted
and devalued when it is not directed at men. We can see
this, for instance, in how bisexual women's relationships
with men are treated as more valid and more defining of
their sexuality than their relationships with women. One
direct impact this has on women in relationships with
women is that they report monitoring the frequency of
sex in the relationship and actively working on increasing their own desire and having sex on a regular basis, regardless of whether they actually want it. Because sex is
associated with intimacy, but also with the validity of a romantic relationship and lesbian or bisexual identity, there
is a pressure on women in relationships with women to

engage in sex they do not want in order to feel secure in both the relationship and their identity.[19]

While some groups are desexualized, others can be hypersexualized and fetishized. This applies, for instance, to black women and men, Asian women, and bisexual people. Hypersexualization is just as harmful to individuals' ability to exercise sexual agency as desexualization, as it makes members of hypersexualized groups more prone to sexual harassment and violence. It also makes it more difficult to access justice for sexual violence, as victims are less likely to be believed and even more likely to be blamed for assault they experience.[20]

## Autonomy?

Dominant discourses about sex, gender, and consent interact with other ways in which subjects are socially constructed and marginalized to shape their sexual choices in a range of ways. The way we think about how men and women *should* experience their sexuality (the male sexual drive discourse, the have/hold discourse, and the permissive discourse) puts pressure on men to seek sex over other types of connection, while putting women in an impossible position trying to reconcile three contradictory demands. The way we define what counts as sex, and how a sexual encounter *should* progress, puts pressure on us to have sex in one particular way that does not work for everyone, as well as excluding some of us from the dominant scripts entirely. And the ways our validity as human beings with full lives and meaningful relationships is tied to our sexuality allow for both desexualization and hypersexualization to be wielded as tools of power. This in turn puts some groups under pressure to "prove" their sexuality while making others more prone to sexual violence.

One result of all of these subtle operations of power is that unwanted (but legally consensual) sex remains remarkably prevalent among people of all genders, in both casual situations and long-term relationships. This highlights the way our choices and available courses of action are shaped by society. It may be tempting to reduce these operations of power to one dimension (gender) and one direction (men oppressing women), and this is the position held by some radical feminists.[21] But it is obvious from the examples discussed in this chapter that reality is much more complex than that. Power is indeed multidirectional and multi-dimensional, and it is impossible to disentangle our apparently autonomous decisions and choices from our social context.

Some feminist philosophers have therefore developed the idea of autonomy in ways that take into account interdependencies and interpersonal relationships, as well as other external factors such as our social and material circumstances, which may shape our choices and actions.

The ways our validity as human beings with full lives and meaningful relationships is tied to our sexuality allow for both desexualization and hypersexualization to be wielded as tools of power.

These approaches are broadly grouped under the heading of relational autonomy. They allow us to see how our relationships with others and our social context can both limit our autonomy but also nurture it.[22] So what does this mean for the idea of autonomy in consent, and particularly for us in that moment where we say yes or no, where we hear our partners' yes or no?

A no, however obliquely expressed, remains a no, and we have an obligation to hear it and act on it. But a genuine respect for our own and others' autonomy puts additional obligations on us. We need to be aware of the operations of power that may shape both our own and our partners' sexual choices. We need to consciously act in ways that do not reproduce those operations of power, and that ideally challenge them. We need to be sensitive to how axes of oppression and marginalization operate and intersect. We need to rewrite sexual scripts, dismantle dominant discourses, and endeavor to level the playing field. How we do this will vary from partner to partner, from situation to situation. In chapter 6, we will examine some of the kinds of activist work going on that seek to do these things on a wider societal scale.

# CULTURE AND CONSENT

**Popular Culture as Sex Education**

Where do we learn about sex and consent? Sex and relationships education for many of us continues to be woefully inadequate. A 2016 report by the Sex Education Forum found that, in the United Kingdom, sexual consent—either as a theory or in discussion of real-life scenarios—is not routinely covered in schools, with a third of young people not being taught anything on the subject at all. Additionally, nearly half of young people are not being taught how to tell a healthy relationship from an abusive one.[1] The situation in the United States is even worse, as debates there are dominated by the question of whether sex and relationships education should cover anything beyond "abstinence only until marriage," with consent barely making it onto the radar in discussions of what is or should be taught.

Some parents are comfortable doing "the talk," but many are not. In fact young people would prefer for their parents to be much more involved in their sex and relationships education than they currently are, and to be one of the main sources of information about sex while growing up.[2] And even parents themselves say they would like to do more for their children on this topic, and be better at it, but feel they lack the skills and confidence.[3] Where parents do give information, for instance about contraception and safer sex practices, their knowledge is frequently inaccurate or out of date,[4] and there is no reason to believe that they are any better equipped to talk about consent.

And of course we don't stop learning about sex and consent once we leave school or become adults. Yet sex advice books and columns aimed at adults have until recently been remarkably silent on the subject, and even in the wake of the #MeToo campaign, advice can be reductive, contradictory, or confusing.

Realistically, we pick up a lot of our knowledge about how sex works, what consent is, and even safer sex practices from the general cultural environment around us, whether by conversing with friends or browsing the internet. But particularly when it comes to things like learning dominant (or possibly alternative) sexual scripts, popular culture plays a very significant role in our sex

Realistically, we pick up a lot of our knowledge about how sex works, what consent is, and even safer sex practices from the general cultural environment around us.

and relationships education, regardless of whether we are young people or adults.

Because culture serves as our main sex educator, it attracts scrutiny and critique in general, and some specific cultural forms have come under fire. There are concerns about the messages contained in everything from romance novels to hardcore pornography about what normal sex, romance, healthy relationships, and consent look like. Feminist activists over the last few years have also drawn attention to a range of problematic tropes reproduced for instance in romantic comedies and popular Christmas songs.[5] In this chapter, then, we will take a look at the role popular culture plays in shaping our ideas of sex, sexuality, and consent. We will specifically examine romance novels, pornography, and sex advice literature, as well as touch on some of the good, the bad, and the ugly from across other forms of culture.

## Pornography

There is a strong and long-lived strand of feminist thought that regards pornography as deeply implicated in the prevalence of sexual and other violence against women. Pornography is seen as inherently degrading and exploitative of women, as normalizing violent sexual practices, and as contributing to the subjugation of women under patriarchy. The argument is that the images presented in pornography are both in themselves violent and that those who consume them are likely to want to reenact them. In this way, radical feminists argue, pornography makes men into rapists and women into willing victims.[6]

While this strand of thought has a history going back to the 1970s, the simplistic causal link between pornography and sexual violence has by and large been discredited.[7] A more recent expression of anti-pornography feminism focuses instead on the ubiquity and accessibility of online pornography specifically, and particularly on its alleged effects on children and young people. Campaigners cite cases of very young children being exposed to pornography, of teenagers sharing nude images of themselves, and of the alleged normalization of sexual practices deemed intrinsically "pornographic," such as anal sex, as examples of pornography's contribution to sexual violence.[8] They claim that the ubiquity of pornography in our culture creates an environment where it is difficult for young people to know what normal, healthy sexual practices and relationships look like, which in turn puts pressure on them to consent to acts they may not want. If you grow up thinking that porn sex is normal sex you may not have the tools to negotiate the kind of sex that works for you.

Over the last decade, campaigners subscribing to these views have had a number of successes in influencing government policy. In the United Kingdom, for instance, there is legislation banning the depiction of a number of sexual acts as "extreme pornography." The government also requires big internet service providers to switch parental controls on by default, and has recently implemented a requirement for pornography websites to be able to verify their users' age, thereby compromising users' anonymity. All this is ostensibly in aid of protecting children from the harmful effects of pornography and from using pornography as a source of (bad) sex education and sexual scripts.

Yet even if we accept that pornography is easy to access and that it may give us sexual scripts and act as a source of knowledge about sex for young people who don't have access to other kinds of sex education, the picture is more complicated than the simple anti-pornography argument would have us believe.

Over the last twenty years or so, there has been a shift in cultural studies from talking about "pornography" to talking about "*pornographies*."[9] This reflects a growing understanding that while some materials are explicitly *produced* with the intention to arouse, a wide range of other types of material are *read* as pornography by individuals, and even among the former category, there is an enormous variety of style, content, and circumstances of production. Pornography, for instance, can be written as well as visual. It can be produced by large mainstream studios or small independent producers, including ones with a feminist and queer outlook. And audiences who may not be able to access what we traditionally think of as pornography may still make pornographic meanings from materials such as women's magazines, advertising, or lingerie catalogs. We cannot reduce the meanings or effects of all of these diverse materials to simple statements such as "this causes violence" or "this reproduces rape culture and limits individuals' ability to negotiate consent." What, then, are some of the possible alternative meanings we make with pornography, and how might they shape our views and relate to our ability to meaningfully consent to sex?

With the proliferation of digital technologies and online distribution, there has been a rise in small, independent pornography producers, particularly ones following a queer and/or feminist ethos. Many of these producers emphasize representation of diverse bodies (in terms, for instance, of race, body type, or disability), different genders (including non-binary ones), sexualities, sexual practices beyond the dominant sexual script, consent, and safer sex practices. They have a strong focus on ethics in both what they choose to depict and in their production processes.[10] Interviews with performers emphasizing the consensual nature of the encounters depicted have become commonplace in queer and feminist pornography.

The audiences for this kind of pornography are disproportionately women and non-binary people of a range of sexual orientations, as well as queer men. Studies of women consumers of queer and feminist pornography indicate that their experiences with this kind of material are complex. How they relate to it, and the meanings they make with it, depend on their attitudes and expectations but also on social factors, and they may experience contradictory emotions ranging from arousal to disgust, all at the same time.[11] These experiences and emotions are in turn used by women viewers to develop their understanding of their own sexuality. They learn to identify and challenge dominant discourses and sexual scripts in both media and their own lives and develop a better sense of their own sexual agency. In this way, some kinds of pornography can function as a way of negotiating one's place within (or outright challenging) rape culture.[12]

Representation in queer and feminist pornography of diverse practices, communities, and body types also has important effects when it comes to consent. It can help counteract some of the discursive operations of power limiting marginalized people's ability to exercise their sexual agency. Particularly groups who are commonly either desexualized (such as fat women) or hypersexualized (such as black women) can find alternative representation in pornography validating and empowering, giving them more confidence in their day-to-day sexual practice and consent negotiation.[13]

Pornography is neither monolithic, nor universally harmful. Viewing it and engaging with it can be a complex, multilayered experience for anyone. Some pornography, for some viewers, may indeed reproduce the dominant sexual scripts that prop up rape culture. Equally though, some types of pornography, for some viewers, can be hugely empowering. It may reflect our identities and experiences, help us explore our sexuality, help us exercise sexual agency and bodily autonomy, and challenge and rewrite dominant scripts of what sex is and how it should work.

It is perhaps ironic, then, that the kind of legislation that anti-pornography feminists campaign for, and that bans "extreme pornography," most severely impacts small and independent producers—the kind more likely to produce queer, feminist, ethical, and consent-focused pornography. The legislation focuses on specific acts: acts that go off the default sexual script, that are more prevalent in queer (and to an extent in feminist) pornography. It casts them as intrinsically deviant and undesirable, regardless of the context of either production or representation. It closes down avenues for challenging default sexual scripts and consensually exploring sexual possibilities beyond that default.[14] This and other similar legislation does not necessarily stop young people—or anyone else—from picking up default sexual scripts from mainstream pornography, and it does nothing to improve education about or understanding of consent.

An alternative and perhaps more constructive approach to the idea that pornography acts as a major source of knowledge and sexual scripts not just for young people but for many in our society has come in the form of sex and relationships education materials. Rather than seeking to ban or restrict access to pornography, this approach seeks to equip young people with the knowledge and resources to explore their own sexuality safely and consensually regardless of any messages they may pick up from pornography or other media.

In 2018, for instance, *Teen Vogue* published an article on anal sex.[15] Consent, as well as inclusivity of queer and trans identities, is at the core of the article. It starts out with a disclaimer for readers who may be uncomfortable reading about the subject and points them at other *Teen Vogue* content they could read instead. It emphasizes consent issues throughout, including the idea that consent should be negotiated beforehand and can be withdrawn at any time. It goes on to dismantle the idea that penile-vaginal intercourse is the only type of sex one could or should be having. Rather than simply dismissing anal sex as an intrinsically deviant, abusive, or "pornographic" practice, it acknowledges that many people genuinely enjoy it. Finally, the article discusses the practicalities of anal sex, while being careful to use gender-neutral language and not make assumptions about who the insertive and who the receptive partner might be. In these ways, it puts images young people may have seen in pornography in the context of real-life sexual experiences and possibilities. It reduces social pressures on them and gives them the space to consider whether some of the sexual practices they see on screen are things they might enjoy without stigmatizing them. It helps young people develop new sexual scripts inclusive of all genders and sexualities in order to negotiate consent and explore their sexuality safely, and with respect for each other's bodily autonomy.

Pornography and its relationship to issues of sexual consent remains a thorny issue. It is a part of our cultural landscape that is here to stay, and like other media it has an effect on how we view sex, consent, and our own sexuality. But it is far from a monolithic cultural phenomenon, and the meanings we make from it are complex and varied. They depend as much on the kinds of pornography we come into contact with as on the other cultural resources we bring with us or have access to. Representations of diversity in independently produced, feminist and queer pornography can also have positive effects on women and queer audiences, strengthening individuals' confidence in their own desires and providing them with new approaches to negotiating consent.

## Romance

Our ideas of what is and is not romantic can shape our behavior in ways that limit our agency, as we saw in some of the examples discussed in chapter 4. Ideas of love and romance are pervasive in our culture, so are there other ways in which they might influence our relationships, the expression of our sexuality, our desires, and our behavior? Romance novels in particular have attracted the attention of feminist scholars and activists for their at times problematic portrayal of sexual and romantic relationships. As romance novels are predominantly aimed at and read by women audiences, the messages they send about what an ideal romantic relationship looks like are a target of feminist scrutiny.

Although queer or LGBT romances have been a niche subgenre within romance novels for decades, and they have become more prominent over the last ten years or so, heterosexual romances make up the bulk of the genre and have as a result garnered the majority of scholarly and activist attention. The first studies of romance novels were written in the 1980s, and were in part a reaction to the "bodice ripper" subgenre of romance novels popular in the 1970s and 1980s, which rightly has a reputation for playing fast and loose with ideas of sexual consent, bodily autonomy, and personal agency. These studies pick up on some of the deeply problematic aspects common to many romance narratives, particularly the hero's behavior toward the heroine.[16]

Romance novels, of course, are primarily about the hero and the heroine overcoming various obstacles to the realization of their love and their "happily ever after" ending in marriage (or more recently, a "happy for now" ending in a long-term committed relationship). Obstacles to love are in fact a formula in our culture that predates the contemporary romance novel genre and industry by centuries. For Romeo and Juliet (who did not have a happily ever after), their feuding families were the obstacle. For Elizabeth Bennet and Mr. Darcy, it was largely a disparity in social standing and wealth. Yet in many modern romance novels the main obstacle is not external to the relationship. Rather, it is the hero's own behavior toward and treatment of the heroine.

The typical romance novel hero in a bodice ripper is frequently gruff and cold, if not downright aggressive, toward the heroine at the outset of the book. In some instances of the romance novel formula, he will even punish the heroine for her initial rejection of him. So how is this obstacle to the couple's alleged true love overcome? Early romance novel scholars argue that in the course of the novel the heroine learns to reinterpret the hero's harsh behavior. Rather than being motivated by cruelty or indifference, the heroine learns, the hero has secretly loved her all along, and all of his acts toward her were motivated by that love. The process of learning and accepting this for the heroine involves an act of self-subversion. She has to challenge her own instincts and interpretations of the hero's behavior in favor of taking his word for what has motivated his cruelty toward her all along.

What messages, then, do the women reading romance novels take away from this? Early popular romance scholars argue that the reader closely identifies with the heroine, and that, as a result, she learns from these books to recode the cruel and aggressive behavior of the men in her own life as a sign of love and affection. According to this view, romance novels help women adapt to (and accept) the demands patriarchy puts on them in their day-to-day lives. In this way, the setting and maintaining of personal boundaries for women—saying "this behavior is not OK" in sexual situations but also in the wider relationship—is discouraged. Abusive behaviors and relationships become not only normalized but are recoded as loving.

And, of course, this trope has wider reach than just romance novels. The idea that "boys will be boys" and show affection to girls by "pulling pigtails"—teasing them and being hurtful—is something children are frequently taught in the playground. Here too, setting and maintaining boundaries is discouraged. So romance novels and the cultural tropes they reproduce are seen as having a negative effect particularly on women's ability to set boundaries in their relationships, which would potentially include negotiating or even withholding or withdrawing sexual consent.

More recently, though, scholars have questioned whether the messages romance novels send are quite so bleak, and whether audiences internalize them as unquestioningly as early accounts would suggest. Readers, after all, can make multiple meanings from the same texts. They can reject or dislike the messages of the genre, or they can interpret them in completely different ways. One recent study has argued that, as romance novels are both written and read predominantly by women, they provide a space in which women can collectively grapple with the challenges that patriarchy poses to them in their lives. In this space, they can reimagine men as freed from patriarchy and toxic masculinity and can look for relationship models in which they are true equals with their partners. This argument is both a reinterpretation of some of the older romance novels, and a reflection of more recent trends and developments in the genre.[17]

Another important factor here is that romance reading is a social activity. Even women featured in early pre-internet studies of romance readers found a community within which they discussed the books they enjoyed.[18] With the advent of social media and social reading sites like goodreads.com, romance-reading communities have only become larger and more diverse. Readers share recommendations and discuss what they do and do not enjoy. Through social media, they also have unprecedented access to authors. In this way, issues that readers care about, including consent, can be thematized and worked through in a communal setting, and new directions for the genre can be set in collaboration between readers and writers.

In fact, consent has become an increasingly hot topic among romance readers and writers, especially following the proliferation of smaller independent romance and erotica publishers enabled in part by the lower costs of publishing ebooks. Authors seek to explicitly depict consent negotiation in their sex scenes, but also to examine unequal power dynamics in relationships and the impact those may have on consent. For a generation of authors who may have grown up reading bodice rippers, this is in part a reaction to that, but also a way to respond to an ongoing conversation in their community, meet reader demands, and move the genre forward.[19] In this way, romance novels and the conversations they spark may actually help rewrite some of our dominant sexual scripts, rather than simply reproducing the tired tropes of rape culture. Of course, not all romance novels do this well, or at all, but there is certainly a section of the community—both readers and writers—that cares deeply about consent and that seeks to redress some of the issues the genre has historically been plagued by.

## Sex Advice

Sex advice has been an integral part of our culture and media landscape for decades now. Sex and relationships advice books such as the classic *Men Are from Mars, Women Are from Venus* are only the tip of the iceberg. Women's magazines, both of the prestige and glossy variety like *Cosmo* and of the gossip variety like *Heat*, have countless pages dedicated to sex advice, and many newspapers' advice columns remain remarkably popular and full of questions about sex. These more traditional sex advice media have been joined by a whole host of online contributions to the genre, offered by media organizations, charities, and individuals on blogs and social networks. So what does sex advice literature have to say on the subject of consent?

The authors of *Mediated Intimacy: Sex Advice in Media Culture*[20] investigated precisely this question by looking at a range of books, newspaper problem pages, and websites, and the results are dispiriting to say the least. Consent as a topic or even index entry is almost completely absent from sex advice books. Not only that, but sex advice literature reproduces many of the problematic and harmful discourses about sex that we discussed in chapter 4, and that make consent such a thorny issue. Like *Men Are from Mars, Women Are from Venus*, many subscribe to the idea that men and women are fundamentally different when it comes to sex, and that men experience a much stronger sex drive. Yet when it comes to talking about how to manage disparities in sexual desire, sex advice literature, particularly for men, frequently encourages coercive and non-consensual behaviors. These can range from mainstream magazines such as *Men's Health* encouraging men to put women under time pressure and question their reasons for refusing sex to niche websites run by "pick-up artists," which read like outright rape manuals.

Mainstream sex advice literature generally subscribes to the "no means no" model of consent: the view that if someone clearly refuses you should not pressure them into sex. By extension, however, this model constructs the absence of a "no" as a "yes." As a result, some experts who dispense sex advice will suggest things like trying out new sexual activities without discussing them first, effectively hoping that you will get away with it. This is problematic in a number of ways and does not encourage an approach to sex and consent that respects others' bodily autonomy. At the same time this literature will also encourage women (especially) to engage in sex even if they do not want it or are not enjoying it—for instance, as a relationship maintenance activity. The juxtaposition of this kind of advice with statements that you should not be coerced into sex may be particularly harmful: it obscures the non-consensual nature of the practices advocated, and makes it more difficult for individuals reading sex advice books and columns to recognize the inherent consent issues involved.

The one context in which mainstream sex advice literature does acknowledge that there may be pressures involved that can affect individuals' ability to freely consent is in the context of sex advice for young people. In particular, online resources aimed at teenagers cover consent in quite a lot of depth and nuance, discussing factors such as drugs and alcohol, social pressures, the relationship-maintenance approach as a kind of pressure, and young people's concerns about appearing immature or juvenile if they do not engage in sex.

The discrepancy between sex advice for young people, which emphasizes social factors and pressures when it comes to consent, and that for adults, which actively reproduces those exact social pressures, is striking. Yet maybe there is a silver lining here, in that today's young people are tomorrow's adults. They will have grown up with much better sex advice when it comes to consent, and therefore hopefully demand a better quality of sex advice for themselves as adults. And we may even be seeing some changes in mainstream sex advice aimed at adults resulting from the #MeToo campaign. One recent *Men's Health* article, for instance, in discussing the idea of "blue balls," specifically addressed the issue of consent.[21] It stated clearly that if your partner withdraws consent, blue balls are not an excuse to keep going, and suggested that masturbation would resolve the issue without violating your partner's bodily autonomy. For a publication that less than five years earlier advocated pressuring women into sex, this is a remarkable turnaround.

## Consent in Wider Popular Culture

Representation and discussion of sex and consent is not limited to particular genres or types of culture. Many products of popular culture have something to say on the subject, even if they are not explicitly pornographic, focused on romance, or seeking to give sex advice. Yet explicit consent negotiation is rarely shown in popular culture. Most of the time all we see is an implied progression through the default sexual script. In film and TV especially, some time after the kissing starts (how long exactly will generally depend on the rating of the product), there is a cut to the next morning with some improbably arranged bed sheets covering everything the censors say needs to be covered (and only that). Where sex is visually implied, it is more often than not penile-vaginal intercourse with little negotiation or consideration of alternatives. In these ways popular culture reproduces and reinforces the dominant sexual script and the primacy of penile-vaginal intercourse as *the* sexual act that "counts." Like other instances and reproductions of this script, this makes it more difficult to imagine and negotiate alternatives that may work better for us as individuals,

Explicit consent negotiation is rarely shown in popular culture. Most of the time all we see is an implied progression through the default sexual script.

taking us instead down one particular path regardless of our consent.

Fortunately, we are beginning to see some exceptions to this monotony of representation, and to the lack of depictions of consent negotiation, though we rarely get both of these in the same product. It is worth considering some specific examples of both developments here, and what they might mean for the possibility of long-term cultural change around consent.

Developments in depicting sexual acts that don't follow the default sexual script tend to be led by TV shows that market themselves as gritty or prestige and are rated for an older audience. They also tend to feature more queer characters and same-gender relationships, both being major vehicles for covering issues of sex beyond the default script. HBO's vampire show *True Blood*, for instance, has both queer representation and some heterosexual scenes that are well outside the bounds of the default sexual script, including representation of BDSM activities. And Netflix's *House of Cards* has at least one memorable scene depicting a man performing cunnilingus.

These developments in how sex is represented in popular culture may allow viewers to begin to think outside the dominant sexual script or validate desires and experiences they have already had in their own lives. Yet the consent negotiation element is absent from them, potentially

Recent developments in how sex is represented in popular culture may allow viewers of some of these shows to begin to think outside the dominant sexual script.

leaving those wishing to go off-script without a clear idea of how to do so.

Where we do tend to see more explicit consent negotiation is in content aimed at young audiences or depicting young adults. At the end of Disney's *Frozen*, for instance, Kristoff shyly asks Anna if he can kiss her. The CW network's recent DC Comics adaptation *Black Lightning* has several extended scenes in which teenage characters Khalil and Jennifer discuss and plan the logistics of having sex for the first time, including a discussion of condom use. Some aspects of this are better executed than others. The way the discussion is framed strongly implies that what they mean by sex is penile-vaginal intercourse, following the dominant sexual script. On the other hand, the conversation takes place outside a sexual situation and the characters are given the opportunity to open up and be vulnerable with each other in admitting their sexual inexperience. A final notable example of consent negotiation depicted on screen is the 2010 film adaptation of the graphic novel *Scott Pilgrim vs. The World*, which contains a scene showing explicit consent withdrawal. Scott and his love interest Ramona are making out after a date when Ramona decides she is not in the mood for this or anything else. Scott respects her choice and the two spend the rest of the night cuddling. Significantly, all these examples provide possible scripts for negotiating consent, including asking for and giving consent, but also withholding or withdrawing consent.

There have also been a few more recent examples of content aimed at an older audience that both challenges the default sexual script and shows explicit consent negotiation. Two of the main characters in ABC's *How to Get Away with Murder*, for instance, are a mixed HIV status gay couple. Once they find out that one of them is HIV-positive, they have to navigate issues of desire, consent, and safer sex practices, including pre-exposure prophylaxis (PrEP). The conversations they have are frank and tend to happen outside of sexual situations, while also acknowledging the role of desire and spontaneity in sex.

Action comedies *Deadpool* and *Deadpool 2* contain two scenes of pegging (anal sex where, in this case, a cisgender woman wearing a strap-on is the insertive partner and a man is the receptive partner), and both contain an element of consent negotiation. In the first, Wade withdraws consent, while in the second he initiates the encounter. Both scenes are in keeping with the extremely tongue-in-cheek tone of the film, showing that consent negotiation does not have to be a serious or legalistic process and can be a fun and integral part of everyday sexual practice. These examples show that a more consent-focused representation of sex and sexuality in popular culture is possible, and can be both entertaining and successful.

We may be seeing some improvements in the representation of sex and consent in popular culture, but there are other ways in which it remains problematic. Particularly when it comes to the representation of marginalized groups and body types, popular culture frequently continues to rely on harmful tropes and construct marginalized subjects as either desexualized or hypersexual in ways that dehumanize them and reproduce some of the more subtle effects of rape culture.

Think, for instance, of Disney's *Moana*. The film features a Disney princess of color who has no love interest or romantic storyline. It is the continuation and extension of a trend seen in films like *Brave* and *Frozen*, where the main characters' goals do not include living "happily ever after" with a man. In *Moana*, there is not even a hint of a romantic relationship for the lead character. The film has received a lot of praise from white feminist critics for this lack of romantic subplot. It shows, they argue, that girls and women can be strong and independent and have adventures of their own, without needing to focus on the prospect of romance, love, or marriage. Critics of color have also praised *Moana* for its representation of Polynesian women, including darker skin, coarse dark hair, and body types that diverge significantly from the slender Disney princess default.

Yet critics of color also express reservations about *Moana*'s lack of a love interest. Some feel that the positive representation of women of color is incomplete or undermined by not showing them leading full lives including sexual and romantic relationships. The underlying message here becomes "yes, you can be dark-skinned, have curly dark hair, and have a body type that does not conform to the slender norm; you might even have great adventures, but ultimately, you will be unlovable."[22]

The core of the disagreement here between white critics and women of color comes down to how race informs dominant ideas of appropriate and acceptable femininity. White femininity is traditionally constructed as delicate, fragile, and dependent on male providers who are to be repaid in romance, love, or sex. For white women, then, strength, independence, and an absence of a love interest in media is perceived as breaking traditional gender roles and therefore liberating and empowering.

But the picture is very different when it comes to dominant ideas of black womanhood. The African American feminist theorist Patricia Hill Collins has identified several dominant "controlling images" of black women present in American culture. The mammy is a desexualized caregiver devoted to her white charges, an image dating back to black women house slaves, whereas the Jezebel is hypersexualized, promiscuous, and aggressive. The two dominant ideas of black motherhood, the matriarch who emasculates and drives away her male partner and the welfare mother who is a single parent, are also notable for denying black women the emotional support of a romantic partnership.[23] Thus for black women, storylines that do not give black women characters a romantic interest, rather than being liberating and empowering, simply reproduce elements of the controlling images and tropes used to exert power over their lives.

We saw in chapter 4 that this becomes an issue in relation to sexual consent because both desexualization and hypersexualization are wielded as instruments of power, used to control and dehumanize some groups of people. And desexualized individuals commonly find it difficult to refuse sexual or romantic advances, or even tend to seek out sex that is otherwise not wanted in order to reaffirm their sexuality. So by offering desexualized representations of women of color, popular culture products like *Moana* reinforce some of the controlling images that limit the ability of women of color to fully exercise agency in their sexual and romantic lives.

The desexualization of black women, in popular culture and elsewhere, also puts asexual and aromantic black people in a double bind: on the one hand, desexualization itself is harmful to allosexual black people, but on the other hand, the resistance to that desexualization frequently takes the form of insisting that sexual and romantic relationships are necessary for a character to be truly fleshed out and leading a full life. This in turn reproduces compulsory sexuality, creating the kind of climate where

We all bring different experiences to our readings of media, resulting in different interpretations. What one person finds empowering may be oppressive to another.

asexual and aromantic people struggle to articulate their experiences and desires and feel pressured to engage in sexual and romantic relationships they may not want.

A lack or representation of healthy romantic relationships also affects groups other than black women. Fat women, disabled people, and older people, among others, are not only desexualized in popular culture but are frequently entirely absent, providing them with even fewer opportunities to see themselves reflected in culture and to draw from it sexual and romantic scripts that help them exercise agency and meaningfully negotiate consent.

Media and popular culture of all kinds does shape the way we think about sex, about our own sexuality, about the kinds of sex we should and should not be having—regardless of our age or sexual experience. But it does this in complex ways that are not reducible to simple cause-and-effect statements. We all bring different experiences to our readings of media, resulting in different interpretations. What one person finds empowering may be oppressive to another. That media effects are complex and highly individualized, however, does not mean that we should not look at media overall critically and seek to understand where it broadly speaking reproduces or challenges harmful dominant discourses and sexual scripts. As a key social institution and source of sexual scripts for most of us, media and popular culture have an important role to play in any future shift from a rape culture to a culture of consent.

# CONSENT KNOWLEDGES, CONSENT ACTIVISMS

## Developing Our Understanding of Consent

Sexual consent continues to be a contested topic in our culture and society. As we have seen in previous chapters, we still live in a rape culture, where the dominant discourses and scripts of how sex *should* work shape our desires and behavior, actively obscure issues of consent, and raise doubts about how freely given consent is in many situations. Our understanding of consent, and what a culture of consent might look like, is still very much developing as we begin to create vocabularies for speaking about experiences that may fall between yes and no, and identify the multi-directional flows of power we are all subject to in our sexual practice.

We might expect the communities generating new knowledge and seeking to expand our understanding of issues of consent to be found predominantly within academia. Feminist academics across a range of disciplines—philosophy, psychology, law, sociology, literature, cultural studies—do have a history of examining this topic and driving knowledge forward, but there are also other communities whose contribution to the area needs to be acknowledged. These communities frequently approach consent from a perspective of lived experience and day-to-day sexual practice, and they bring a range of tools to the table that are not necessarily available (or perhaps sufficiently respectable) within the confines of academia. In this chapter, therefore, we will explore where cutting-edge thought on consent comes from today. We will see that the line between knowledge creation and activism is frequently blurred, as finding the vocabulary to challenge dominant discourses is a first and necessary step toward creating lasting change.

## Consciousness-Raising, Online and Off

Feminist thinkers and campaigners have known for a long time that our lived experience is an invaluable source of knowledge. But that lived experience is also frequently filtered through the dominant discourses of our society. These discourses can obscure what is really going on and leave us with a feeling that something is "off" without being able to put our finger on it. Without support from a community, this experience can leave us feeling isolated, as if something is wrong with *us* rather than with the world at large. The feminist practice of consciousness-raising aims to provide that community support and help individuals re-evaluate and make sense of their lived experience in new ways.

Consciousness-raising originated in feminist communities in the 1960s in the United States. It started in small groups that met face to face, frequently in someone's house. They would talk about the issues they experienced in their own lives, finding that they were far from alone, and rather than being personal and individual, these issues were social and systemic. This process contributed strongly to the formulation of feminist thought on issues such as reproductive rights, domestic work, and domestic violence. It is a practice that has evolved over the years, but it continues to be used today to develop knowledge and understanding of many issues, including sexual consent.

Technological change has been a key factor in how feminist consciousness-raising practice has evolved. The internet, and particularly social media, has provided a platform for feminist voices to speak out and reach a much wider audience than any face-to-face consciousness-raising group could. There are vibrant feminist communities all over the internet, producing blog posts, Twitter threads, and elaborate and in-depth conversations. Over the last ten years or so, consent has become one of the key issues taken up by these communities.

Like with traditional consciousness-raising groups, one key activity in feminist online communities is the sharing of individual lived experience. Survivors of sexual violence frequently share their stories. Some are only able to do so under the protection of online anonymity, but we are increasingly seeing individuals—both celebrities and otherwise—share their stories openly and publicly under their real names. Individual accounts like these both humanize victims and survivors and make visible the diversity of circumstances and sexual violence experiences.

In this way, they challenge common rape myths. We see that rape and sexual assault happens to people who were not wearing short skirts, were not walking alone in a deserted area at night. We see that it happens to people who were doing those things, too, which does not make it any less wrong or any more their fault. These accounts also allow other victims and survivors to see reflections of themselves in these stories, validating their own feelings and experiences. They may even help reframe one's understanding of an experience, or name something as a violation that had always felt slightly off but that the person may not have had the words for. In this way, sexual violence is no longer framed as the personal tragedy of isolated individuals but as a pervasive social problem.

This kind of online (and offline) consciousness-raising activity is in fact part of the origin of the #MeToo campaign. While the hashtag and associated campaigns gained

Survivors of sexual violence frequently share their stories. Individual accounts like these both humanize victims and survivors and make visible the diversity of circumstances and experiences. In this way, sexual violence is no longer framed as the personal tragedy of isolated individuals but as a pervasive social problem.

widespread media attention in late 2017 and early 2018, "me too" has been a rallying cry of sexual assault survivors for over a decade. Tarana Burke, an African American feminist and civil rights activist, coined the phrase in 2006 precisely as a way of giving voice to lived experience and drawing attention to the ubiquity of sexual violence in an effort to help survivors.

Consciousness-raising allows not only for experiences to be shared and validated, but also for insights and theory to be generated from them. When a person shares a story about feeling under pressure to have sex, for instance, and others validate it, we can begin to speculate about the precise nature and origins of those pressures. The three discourses of (hetero)sex discussed in chapter 4 (the male sexual drive, have/hold, and permissive discourse) were elaborated as a result of precisely such consciousness-raising groups.[1] They have been crucial in developing our understanding of the social pressures we can sometimes feel that impact and limit our agency in sexual situations. More recently, discussions on feminist blogs and social media have enabled us to challenge the "no means no" model of consent and propose more positive and active models such as enthusiastic consent, or sex-critical models that take social pressures and power differentials into account.

The idea of compulsory sexuality that we touched on in chapter 4 was also largely proposed and elaborated through consciousness-raising activities by the growing online asexual community. Asexual people found online spaces where they could gather and share their experiences of the social pressures they felt to be sexual, or to have sex, even if they did not want it. They discussed the effect those pressures had on them: for instance, in pushing them toward having or even initiating unwanted sex with partners who assumed that any romantic relationship also had to be sexual. They also highlighted the social costs of resisting those pressures, such as consistently having their identity invalidated and dismissed, being dehumanized, and struggling to establish the kinds of relationships they wanted. These shared experiences allowed the community to build on the existing feminist concept of compulsory heterosexuality and to articulate the idea of compulsory sexuality. And as we have seen, compulsory sexuality, a concept developed largely through consciousness-raising, is very useful in thinking about issues of consent and the effect of power relations and social pressures on our desires and behavior.

Another important function of consciousness-raising is the teaching of practical skills. Face-to-face groups and workshops, feminist zines, and online spaces frequently dedicate time and space to this. Participants learn from each other, in a non-hierarchical way, with everyone contributing their own experiences and insights to an open discussion. In this way, they can develop skills around understanding their own boundaries and desires, asking for consent, respecting others' boundaries, as well as giving, withholding, or withdrawing consent. This can help challenge and counteract deeply internalized attitudes and myths. People coming across these spaces for the first time frequently speak of the transformational effect they can have on their understanding of themselves and their sexual history and agency.[2]

Both online and offline, this kind of experience sharing, learning, and knowledge development happens in conversation. Individuals add their own stories, validate each other's feelings and experiences, express sympathy, and give advice. In this way, feminist communities create and spread knowledge about consent collaboratively, building on each other's contributions. This process ensures that knowledge is never complete—we can always improve our understanding, develop concepts further, and peel back more and more layers of rape culture. We can also, in a caring and compassionate way, help new members of feminist communities go through a learning process and make their own contributions.

The knowledges of consent that online and offline feminist communities create through consciousness-raising and similar activities are rooted in individuals' own lived experiences. Understanding, questioning, and theorizing our lived experience of sexuality, consent, and the operations of power that impact us in these areas is a key tool for both knowledge creation and activism. Doing so in a supportive and compassionate community setting is invaluable, as it validates our feelings and allows us to see the bigger picture of social and systemic issues, not just our own personal, individualized problems.

## Practical Steps toward Decentering the Law

We know from crime statistics that the criminal justice system is woefully inadequate in addressing sexual violence, with studies showing that in countries such as the United Kingdom, Canada, the United States, and Australia, less than 10 percent of rapes reported to the police result in a conviction.[3] Taking into account the fact that the majority of cases of sexual violence continue to go unreported, this means that only a tiny percentage of all cases results in any kind of consequences for the perpetrator. As we saw in chapter 2, as well as not being effective in delivering justice, the legal system frequently re-traumatizes victims, and legislation does not actually appear to value human sexuality, agency, autonomy, and integrity. There is, as a result of all these factors, a strand within feminist legal theory and activism that advocates not legal reform, but decentering and sidestepping the law entirely in our attempts to address issues of sexual violence.[4]

There are also other reasons why we might want to avoid getting the state involved in cases of sexual violence and consent violation. For many victims, including sex workers, migrants, trans people (especially trans women), other queer people, and people of color, turning to the police may not be safe. And that fact alone, as well as other social and structural factors that marginalize these groups, means that they are disproportionately affected by sexual violence.

Authorities frequently dismiss sex workers' complaints of sexual violence, and sex workers may end up themselves being criminalized, incarcerated, or losing their livelihood if they attempt to report sexual violence to the police. Migrants, regardless of whether documented or not, may find themselves the targets of immigration enforcement. Trans women may be misgendered and seen as men by law enforcement, which in turn may lead to them being disbelieved, especially if their attackers are cisgender women. Trans women who are also sex workers risk being criminalized and incarcerated in men's prisons. Queer people may be disbelieved, especially if their attackers are the same gender as them.

Finally, communities of color are systematically over-policed and over-incarcerated in many Western countries. For many black men in the United States, contact with the police may be lethal, as we have seen in countless news stories over the last five years. In fact, there is a long history of allegations of black men's sexual violence against white women being used as a pretext for terrorizing

For many victims, including sex workers, migrants, trans people (especially trans women), other queer people, and people of color, turning to the police may not be safe.

black communities through the practice of lynching (whereas white men's violence against both black and white women continues to go unchallenged).[5] It is understandable, therefore, that these communities would not want to invite the police into their lives, both because of the risk to them as victims but also because of the disproportionate risk to perpetrators.

Some communities, particularly intersectional feminists, prison abolitionists, and anarchists, have therefore started thinking about how sexual violence and consent violations can be addressed without getting the law involved, and putting into practice processes rooted in ideas of transformative justice. Transformative justice is an evolving framework that seeks to repair any harm caused by a transgression rather than punish a perpetrator. It does this through voluntary processes that foster dialogue and understanding while providing support for all parties involved. Some approaches within this tradition also pay attention to and seek to redress the structural causes of issues as well as prevent recurrence of the same issues.[6]

In transformative justice, an accountability process replaces the criminal justice trial. Accountability processes may vary, but in many, a complainant who makes an allegation is provided with a support team from among the community. The perpetrator is also provided with a support group and asked to agree to participate in the process. Participation is voluntary. The process may give both parties the opportunity to air their concerns, or focus on working with perpetrators to help them understand the harm they have caused and take steps to change their behavior. Outcomes of this process may include perpetrators accepting that they have caused harm and apologizing for it, and committing to take specific actions to reduce the likelihood of future harm, such as attending consent workshops, learning about rape culture, or disclosing their history of boundary violation to future partners.

Such disclosure is one of the most challenging ideas coming from transformative justice approaches to sexual violence. Some groups have even created materials to help individuals do this.[7] The idea of such public and ongoing accountability may seem daunting, but it does emphasize that learning about consent and shedding rape culture is a lifelong endeavor for all of us, and that we all have the potential to change and improve our consent practice.

Transformative justice approaches have several advantages over the criminal justice system. The stakes and possible consequences for the accused are much less severe, while also having the potential to be genuinely transformational and help them change their attitudes and behavior. Perpetrators may still be defensive and reject the process, but equally they may be helped by other community members to take accountability for their actions. Transformative justice is much less adversarial than criminal justice, instead encouraging dialogue and understanding. It does not seek to determine one version of truth, instead focusing on individuals' lived experience and the harm caused. As a result of this, it is in a much better position to deliver not only justice but also healing to survivors of sexual assault. Offenders remain integrated in the community throughout, rather than being isolated and then having to be "rehabilitated," as happens in the criminal justice system. Finally, because transformative justice seeks to address systemic issues as well as specific harm, it is much more likely to contribute toward a culture of consent than the criminal justice system, which frequently reproduces rape culture.

Nevertheless, there are a number of problems with transformative justice. The biggest is perhaps that it is disproportionately resource-intensive and time-consuming for the small communities that practice it, and it is currently uncertain how transformative justice would scale beyond those communities. It may also be unclear what success actually looks like, and communities may lack the skills to conduct the process as well as the ways to ensure compliance with the outcomes that result from it. And of course because we are all steeped in a society with an adversarial criminal justice system, it is impossible for transformative justice processes to not be tainted by the attitudes and problems that come with that.

Yet communities practicing transformative justice are making significant contributions to our understanding of consent issues and, crucially, to developing non-adversarial, non-punitive alternative frameworks for dealing with those who violate others' boundaries and bodily autonomy.

## The Margins of Normality

One of the key insights from research on sex advice and consent is that in the rare instances when mainstream sex advice does cover consent, it is almost exclusively in the context of BDSM practices.[8] One effect this has is to mark out the boundaries between "normal sex" and "abnormal sex." In this way "normal sex"—penile-vaginal intercourse between a non-disabled cisgender man and a non-disabled cisgender woman, maybe accompanied by some activities labeled "foreplay"—is constructed as something that does not require explicit consent negotiation. The assumption is that we all know how to follow the default sexual script, we can all just easily say yes or no, and hear and respect consent or non-consent when it comes to "normal sex."

On the other hand, "abnormal sex"—such as BDSM, which in this context frequently stands in for any practices diverging from the default script—is constructed as needing special precautions, most commonly in the form of safewords. What mainstream sex advice does not mention is that safewords are only one among many consent practices common in BDSM communities, that those practices apply to "normal sex" just as much as they do to "abnormal sex," or that consent (in BDSM and otherwise) is not just a straightforward transaction between rational individuals but is shaped by our social circumstances and power relations. So what can sex constructed as abnormal teach us about consent?

BDSM communities have been undergoing significant changes in outlook and understanding of consent issues over the last ten years.[9] Because BDSM play is commonly constructed as "abnormal sex," practitioners within BDSM communities have historically been aware that what they do can be seen by outsiders as abusive, and this is one of the reasons why consent has been a focus in these communities for a long time. Because BDSM practices are socially stigmatized, the communities that have grown around them have also adopted a "sex-positive" approach, which includes the underlying assumption of individual freedom and agency. Consent, then, has largely been understood as negotiated between rational individuals unencumbered by power relations. Little thought or time has historically been devoted to the social structures and conditions within communities that might limit individuals' ability to meaningfully and freely negotiate consent.

A certain kind of defensive attitude toward external accusations of abuse has led some BDSM communities in the past to deny that abuse was possible within them, and to emphasize consent negotiation and practices such as safewording when discussing their practices outside the scene.

This has changed over the last ten years, with many community members speaking out about abuses they have experienced and witnessed.[10] Conversations in online spaces dedicated to BDSM have turned toward understanding and challenging the structural issues and operations of power within BDSM scenes that may enable and protect abusers and silence victims. BDSM communities are steeped in the same rape culture as the rest of us, so it is perhaps not surprising that they experience the same problems in this regard as society at large. Because of dominant discourses around personal responsibility and consent as an individualized negotiation, for instance, abuse victims frequently feel like what they experienced was their fault, down to their own failure to clearly communicate non-consent. But there are also problems that are specific to BDSM communities. Individuals may feel that not consenting to a particular practice may mark them out as not cut out for BDSM. Help outside the community can be hard to access due to a combination of social stigma and the difficulty of explaining the complexities of consenting to some practices but not others to those not versed in consent issues. At the same time the community itself can close ranks around the abuser to protect its own reputation and self-image.

As a result, some BDSM communities have developed nuanced understandings of issues of power, community structures, and behavioral norms in consent. Discussions of consent have moved from the notion of individualized negotiation to putting responsibility for consent and safety on the wider community. Communities as a whole have been working on removing pressures on individuals to consent to acts they are uncomfortable with and on creating structures and norms that make it easier to withhold or withdraw consent. They have also tried to put in place ways of ensuring consent decisions are respected, victims of abuse are believed and supported, and those who violate boundaries face consequences.

For example, individuals new to the community are made aware not only of the possible ways in which ability to consent may be impacted by community norms but also of ways to ensure they respect others' boundaries and bodily autonomy. Including explicit, specific, and audience-visible consent negotiation in demonstrations and classes on BDSM practices is another way to normalize consent practices within the scene.[11] In these ways, BDSM communities, while far from perfect, are seeking to create the conditions in which someone can say no, which in turn make any yes freely given and meaningful.

This awareness of power relations and social structures and their effect on individual agency, along with practical ways to mitigate that effect, has been a key contribution of BDSM communities to recent developments in our understanding of consent. With that in mind, it is perhaps ironic that BDSM practices and communities gained media attention following the publication of EL James's *Fifty Shades* series of novels and subsequent film adaptations.

The books, labeled by media and critics as "mommy porn," were a publishing sensation, topping bestseller lists and generating countless column inches of commentary about the popularity of sexually explicit content with women readers. They follow ingénue and virgin Anastasia Steele as she meets and develops a relationship with millionaire Christian Grey. Christian introduces Ana to the world of BDSM, demanding that she become his submissive, with their erotic exploits and developing romance taking up 1,500 pages over three novels, with additional novels recounting the same events from Christian's point of view. The popularity of the books propelled BDSM practices and communities into the public consciousness, something many actual BDSM practitioners have been less than happy about.

The handling of consent in the *Fifty Shades* series has been the key target of criticism, from feminist activists both within and outside BDSM communities. They have pointed out a number of abusive behaviors that are portrayed in the book as normal and romantic. Christian has Ana sign a consent contract and non-disclosure agreement of their relationship, isolating her from friends and other potential sources of support should anything go wrong in their relationship. He demands (and in many cases gains) control of her reproductive choices, her exercise regime and diet, and other details of her day-to-day life. Christian consistently overrides Ana's consent decisions, both sexual and non-sexual, to the point where he punishes her for using her safeword. Ana and Christian's relationship is a much better representation of a toxic, abusive situation than of a BDSM arrangement.

BDSM communities have made considerable efforts to distance themselves from the books and educate the wider public about the problems with the novels, and about consent practices within the community.[12] This has been a key vehicle for ideas about consent developed in BDSM circles permeating into other activist communities, though arguably it has been less successful in reaching the general public. Yet with consent issues becoming more prominent in public discourse, we are beginning to see some of these ideas reflected in more mainstream discussions, showing how valuable knowledges about consent created at the margins of "normal" sex can, at least slowly and partially, reach a wider audience.

## Exploring Consent through Fiction

We saw in chapter 5 that some kinds of pornography can and do engage with issues of ethics in both production and audience engagement, and that as a result they can help shed light on issues of consent. This can happen, for instance, through representations of genders and sexualities outside the cisgender, heterosexual norm, or through showcasing diverse body types that are commonly either desexualized or hypersexualized. In this way, sexually explicit material can create a space for challenging dominant ideas about what sex is and how it should work. But commercial pornography (whether mainstream or independent) is not the only type of sexually explicit material that can be used to explore issues of consent.

One community that produces written pornographic stories and has a long history of using them to think about sexual consent is the fanfiction community. Fanfiction stories are written by amateur writers and based on existing cultural products such as TV series, books, video games, or films. These writers enjoy their favorite fictional characters and settings so much that they create new stories for them. Depending on who you ask, fanfiction either originated with stories based on the original series of *Star Trek* in the 1960s and 1970s, or it has been around since, at the very least, the classical canon, with Virgil's *Aeneid* being fanfiction of Homer's *Iliad*, the Arthurian legend being fanfiction of the *Aeneid*, and so on. Contemporary fanfiction is written mostly by women and non-binary people, the majority of whom identify as queer in some way.[13] It is circulated non-commercially, generally online. For a variety of reasons, a large percentage of this kind of fiction is erotic or sexually explicit, and a significant proportion of it deals with same-gender relationships.[14]

Like BDSM practices, the fanfiction community started attracting public attention with the publication of James's *Fifty Shades of Grey* series, which originated as a piece of fanfiction for Stephanie Meyers's *Twilight* series. But the community is considerably older than that, and has a history of shunning the limelight, for two reasons. First, the status of fanfiction in relation to copyright law has long been regarded as legally murky at best, and many rights holders of the originary works that have inspired fanfiction stories have historically objected to the practice, sending cease-and-desist letters to authors and hosting websites and threatening lawsuits.[15] Second, the fact that fanfiction is often an expression of women's and queer sexualities, which in turn are socially stigmatized, patholo-gized, dismissed, and ridiculed by mainstream culture, has made most readers and writers in this community wary of public attention. Thus, we have a community largely hidden away from public scrutiny, consisting mostly of queer women and non-binary people, producing millions of words about sex for each other, without the pressures that commercial cultural production is under. How, then, does this community approach issues of sexual consent?

One interesting feature of fanfiction in this regard is that, because so much of it focuses on same-gender relationships, it cannot build on the default cis- and heteronormative sexual script. As we have seen in chapters 4 and 5, when there is not exactly one penis and exactly one vagina attached to a cisgender man and a cisgender woman, respectively, there is less of a linear path to follow from drinks to kissing to touching to a particular sexual act that is defined as the only one that counts. And while alternative sexual scripts do exist in queer cultures, the characters in these stories have more latitude to openly and explicitly negotiate what they want to do. Fanfiction readers and writers report that this allows them to notice and challenge the operation of dominant sexual scripts in their own lives, as well as actively rewrite those scripts in ways that offer room for consent negotiation and exploration, and for expanding their understanding of intimacy and sex.

Another very common element of erotic fanfiction stories is the focus on relationships with significant power differentials between the characters. These relationships may play out as romance tropes like marriages of convenience, where one partner is socially and financially dependent on the other, or relationships between superiors and subordinates in a work context, or they might take place in elaborately crafted, shared science-fictional universes with completely different genders and social structures to the ones we are familiar with.

These settings allow fanfiction readers and writers to explore the role of power in intimate relationships and consent negotiation. For instance, can a character completely financially dependent on a partner really say no? And if not, then to what extent is any consent given, even if it is a genuine yes, truly meaningful? What would need to be true for such a relationship to become a level playing field? And whose responsibility is it to create the conditions where "no" can both be said and heard? These are some of the questions these stories pose and try to answer. They show characters negotiating the disjunctures between dominant sexual scripts and their own desires, and they show partners with more power in a relationship taking responsibility for and putting work into making sure that any consent given is indeed given freely.[16]

The fanfiction community has even come up with a word for all of those situations where consent is not a clear-cut yes or no: *dubcon*, short for "dubious consent." Dubcon as a concept helps make visible the fact that there isn't always a sharp dividing line between "rape" and "consent." There is, as we have seen in chapter 4, a vast grey area in between, where the multi-directional flows of power in our culture and society can make individual decisions less than clear-cut. There are situations where sex may be genuinely wanted and yet a person may not be in a position to freely give consent. In others, sex may not be wanted for itself and yet consent may still be freely given for other reasons. Fanfiction uses "dubcon" as an umbrella term to explore all of these and more. It pays attention to characters' internal feelings and experiences, and looks at situations from multiple angles, in ways that emphasize the emotional messiness and lived reality of human sexuality.

One final important aspect of how the fanfiction community explores issues of sexual consent is the way members present their texts and talk about them. A fanfiction text does not stand on its own; rather, it is woven into a fabric of other texts: the work it is based on, for example, or other fanfiction stories, common genre tropes, and conversations between readers and writers. It is created, circulated, and interpreted within a community, and that community has developed a set of shared practices around consent. Community members use the technical tools (such as tags) intended to make stories searchable and discoverable on archive websites in innovative ways to continue the discussion on consent around the text. By using tags, stories that explore the emotional impact of rape, or those that deal with dubious consent, can also be flagged as such so that readers know what they are getting into; this gives them the opportunity to consent (or not) to engaging with the material. In this way, the community not only further develops its own understanding of consent issues but also transforms it into action: a kind of praxis of consent, a living and practicing of the knowledges developed, that permeates the community's technical infrastructure and behavioral norms.

Fanfiction, then, can be used as a tool to think through consent issues in ways that put an emphasis on the internal, emotional experience of sexuality. The sexual fantasy becomes a way of exploring options, making visible social structures and default scripts, and offering potential alternatives that would allow us to build a culture of consent. It is similar to the other forms of knowledge production and activism discussed in this chapter, in that they all use tools to think about issues of consent that are not available, or not sufficiently respectable, to those in academia. Feminist and queer consciousness-raising activities build on lived experience, transformative justice approaches reject and find ways of sidestepping the law, and BDSM communities use their position at the margins of normality to question dominant discourses and make visible things that otherwise we take for granted. These communities are actively extending our collective understanding of what consent means, how rape culture affects our agency and autonomy, and what a true culture of consent might look like.

# #METOO—NOW WHAT?

## Supporting Survivors and Beyond

When the African American activist Tarana Burke coined the phrase "me too" in 2006, she was seeking to give victims of sexual violence a voice, and a way to relate to each other. She calls this "empowerment through empathy": when survivors exchange that phrase, they say to each other, "I believe you, I know what you are going through." In a culture that systematically disbelieves victims of sexual violence, that one phrase in and of itself wields immense power.[1] Burke's organization was set up to help and support survivors of sexual violence, particularly young women of color in her community, and later expanded its remit to people of all genders and ages. With its newfound global visibility, Burke has expressed concerns that the message of the #MeToo movement is getting derailed and diluted.[2]

As is the nature of many social and political movements in the age of social media, #MeToo is not so much
one single, unified force, as millions of diverse, independent voices in dialogue with each other. As a result, it does
not necessarily offer one single or cohesive solution to the
problem of sexual violence. But there are some key strands
emerging from the countless conversations and discussions. As Tarana Burke has repeatedly reminded us, a focus on supporting victims and survivors of sexual violence
is crucial. Not only that, but we need to ensure the most
vulnerable and marginalized of victims are at the center of
these efforts.

But to eradicate sexual violence, to dismantle rape
culture and build a culture of consent, we need to work
toward fundamental social change. #MeToo has enabled
survivors—silenced and stigmatized for years—to speak
out in public. But the stigma is still there, and the disbelief
and silencing have not gone away. There *are* indications
that some things are changing. It has become slightly (but
only slightly) harder to dismiss victims. Some (but only
some) perpetrators are being made to face consequences.
There has been some (limited) change in legislation and in
legal practitioners' approach to sexual violence cases. And
the issue of consent—what it is, how it works—has made
headlines (some positive, others less so). Discussions of
consent have also raised the question of power—both the
obvious abuses of power of people like Harvey Weinstein

As is the nature of many social and political movements in the age of social media, #MeToo is not so much one single, unified force, as millions of diverse, independent voices in dialogue with each other.

and Donald Trump, and the more insidious, day-to-day operations of power that we looked at in chapter 4.

All of which begs the question: Where do we go from here? What does long-term, sustainable, meaningful change look like? How do we dismantle rape culture? How do we build a culture of consent? And what are the pitfalls along the way?

Rape culture and the pervasiveness of sexual violence in our society are underpinned by both legal and cultural factors. As we have seen, feminist legal theorists have long argued that the law treats rape like a property crime rather than something that infringes on our autonomy, integrity, and basic humanity. They have also pointed out other issues with legislation, as well as the way the law is put into practice, that ultimately lead to a failure on the part of the criminal justice system to tackle sexual violence. At the same time, rape myths, the pushing or ignoring of boundaries, discourses about what "normal" sex looks like, who gets to have it and how, are pervasive in our culture. In some cases, they outright limit how meaningful and free our consent can be. In others, these operations of power subtly shape our desires and behaviors in ways that are toxic and harmful. And of course there are countless survivors of sexual violence who need support, healing, and justice. So if we want to achieve meaningful change and dismantle rape culture, we have to tackle all these areas.

## Legal Reform

The importance of legal reform has historically been contested in feminist legal theory and campaigning. On the one hand, a series of campaigns have achieved gains such as the criminalization of marital rape and improvements to how the criminal justice system treats victims and survivors. On the other hand, these changes have not necessarily resulted either in a higher conviction rate for sexual violence or in a reduction of sexual violence. There are also serious questions to be asked about the overall role of the criminal justice system in reproducing multiple other forms of oppression in addition to rape culture. Legal reform, therefore, cannot be the only pillar of a campaign for lasting change, but there are specific changes we may want to see implemented to bring the criminal justice system closer to a state where it is fit for purpose when it comes to sexual violence.

The legal definition of rape is one area where change is still needed in many jurisdictions. At the time of writing, only eight European countries recognize all nonconsensual sex as rape, and three of these (Germany, Iceland, and Sweden) have only in the last two years changed their laws to remove certain factors, such as additional force or physical resistance on the part of the victim, from the definition.[3] French law requires violence, constraint, threat, or surprise rather than the absence of consent to recognize a rape. Norwegian law requires violence or threats, or the victim to be incapable of resisting, as does Swiss law. In most European countries, no does not mean no. Working toward consent-centric definitions of rape and other sexual offenses, therefore, is a vital step in improving the criminal justice system's handling of sexual violence. Additionally, where consent-centric definitions of rape exist, they need to consider the realities of consent negotiation and the operations of power in our society. Requiring affirmative consent—a clear yes rather than the absence of no—should be a key part of such definitions, as should the ability to withdraw consent at any time.

Yet even in jurisdictions with consent-centric definitions of rape, victims who report rape and sexual assault to the police continue to be mistreated and re-traumatized by the criminal justice system, while their attackers frequently get away. Feminist campaigners have achieved a number of improvements in the treatment of victims by the law across many jurisdictions. In the United Kingdom, for instance, these include anonymity for complainants, changes to the way they can be asked to appear in court, such as testifying behind a screen, and a ban on discussing complainants' sexual history as part of the trial (with certain exemptions).

But the experience of reporting sexual assault and testifying in court remains traumatic. In a high-profile trial of two professional rugby players and two other men in

Northern Ireland in 2018, the complainant was asked to give evidence over eight days and was cross-examined by four separate defense lawyers, to jeers and laughter from the public gallery in the courtroom. The defense argued, among other things, that the victim's lack of physical resistance or screaming indicated consent, and that her internal injuries were no clear proof of vaginal intercourse having taken place. Despite this ordeal and the harrowing details of the case, all four defendants were acquitted.[4]

Further reforms to how sexual assault victims are treated by the criminal justice system—from reporting to trial and beyond—are therefore urgently needed. Victims are let down in many jurisdictions, in one way at least, because they are not actually represented by a legal team. Rather, in countries such as the United Kingdom and Canada, victims act as a witness for the prosecution. This drastically limits the support available to them and thrusts them into a hostile and confrontational environment with little preparation; defense lawyers are trained to use such situations to their own advantage. As a result, rape myths, and particularly myths about what does and does not constitute consent, continue to be reproduced in courtrooms, as happened in the Northern Irish rugby case.[5] Even where consent-centric legal definitions of rape exist, in the hands of a skilled defense lawyer pitted against an unsupported victim, consent becomes a meaningless concept. Support for victims throughout the legal process, from professionals who have had comprehensive training on issues of consent, rape culture, and rape myths, could make a significant difference here.

Another key area of victims' interaction with the criminal justice system in need of improvement is the collection and processing of forensic evidence. There is a perception that DNA evidence is key to the outcome of rape trials, and as a result victims who report rape to the police, particularly those who do so soon after it has occurred, are routinely asked to submit to rape kit examinations. Rape kit processes are invasive and can be traumatic, especially following already existing trauma. Yet over the last ten years it has emerged that the United States has a rape kit backlog (forensic evidence that has been collected but either not sent in for analysis or not analyzed by the lab in a timely manner) in the hundreds of thousands.[6]

It is also questionable to what extent rape kit evidence makes a difference to the outcome of rape trials at all. Although it can potentially help identify an unknown attacker, the vast majority of victims of sexual assault know the perpetrator. Moreover, forensic evidence rarely has anything to say about the key issue of consent. So, although in some cases it may prove that sexual contact with a particular person occurred, it cannot shed any light on whether that contact was consensual or not. Rape kits have a minimal if any impact on the outcome of the vast majority of rape cases.[7] Rethinking both the need for and the process of forensic evidence collection would therefore be a key step in improving the treatment of victims by the law.

Any legal reform campaign on sexual violence needs to examine as well how the legal system reproduces not only rape culture but also other existing forms of oppression, such as racism, heteronormativity and queerphobia, and other social inequalities, which affect the treatment of both victims and defendants. Domestic and sexual violence where victim and perpetrator are of the same gender is one area where dominant ideas about gender and what such violence looks like are reproduced. Police and prosecutors may not believe victims whose attacker is of the same gender, or they may blame and stigmatize the victims further.[8]

Rape victims from poorer backgrounds, as well as black and brown victims, also struggle to get their cases prosecuted. Police and prosecutors are more likely to probe their criminal records and question their credibility.[9] As a result, many victims are reluctant to report their experiences to the police in the first place: in the United States, 80 percent of reported rapes are reported by white women, despite the fact that white people make up 64 percent of the US population, and that black, indigenous, and mixed-race women are more likely to be assaulted than white women.[10]

At the same time, black, brown and/or Muslim men are more likely to be prosecuted, especially for sexual violence against white women, than white men, and their violence is more likely to be publicly linked to their race or religion. One member of parliament in the United Kingdom in 2017 claimed that men of Pakistani origin were disproportionately involved in "grooming gangs," yet evidence of that is inconclusive at best.[11] The law, and its uses by those in power, is far from neutral in the ways it is applied, in sexual violence cases and beyond, and in the face of that consent becomes a secondary concern.

The criminal justice system has a long history not only of letting down victims of sexual violence but also of reproducing other forms of oppression and inequalities. This needs to be addressed before it can be considered fit for purpose in dealing with issues of sexual violence. In the longer term, a focus on transformative justice rather than punishment may be a significantly more appropriate way for the law to tackle sexual violence than its current approaches.

### Cultural Change

Legal reform alone (whether in terms of legislation or legal practice) cannot dismantle rape culture or create a culture of consent. To do that, we need to address the role that

The criminal justice system has a long history not only of letting down victims of sexual violence but also of reproducing other forms of oppression and inequalities.

culture plays in reproducing rape myths and dominant ideas about sex, gender, and power. It may be tempting to think that consent is a matter of individuals negotiating their desires and boundaries, but in a rape-supportive cultural environment such negotiation is frequently not conducted freely or on equal terms. Culture here can mean both popular culture such as music, television, or films, and our day-to-day practices and the beliefs we hold about everything from personal and collective responsibility to what behaviors are appropriate for people of what genders.

One starting point for cultural transformation is to expand our idea of consent beyond the sexual. A true culture of consent would permeate our lives in everyday situations and interactions outside the bedroom. This can apply to how we interact within our friendship groups and families, with our colleagues, and with complete strangers. We have probably all nagged our friends to join us for an outing they would have rather missed. We may have been put in awkward situations that demanded we hugged people we would have rather stayed away from. At the same time, most of us do not have access to the scripts to ask for consent in social situations, or to respond to such requests. We need to find ways of normalizing offering someone a hug (as well as them accepting or refusing that offer). We need to become more attentive to refusals, whether they are subtle or direct.

A second key building block of consent culture is becoming attentive to and dismantling the operations of power through discourse that prop up rape culture. We need to better understand how compulsory sexuality operates and is leveraged against marginalized groups. We also need to continue interrogating traditional gender roles and dominant discourses about sexuality, and dismantle dominant ideas about what "normal" sex looks like, what "counts" as sex, and how we "should" be having sex.

Another important area to consider in terms of cultural practices is what we teach children and young people about bodily autonomy and consent in day-to-day life—both through conversations and formal education, but also through how we treat them. Very young children's bodily autonomy, for instance, is severely limited both by their own abilities and by some of our social norms around what is and is not appropriate in interacting with a child. Of course, sometimes finding a balance between giving as much autonomy as possible to children and caring for them can be hard. Brushing teeth, taking medicine, wearing clothing appropriate for the weather, and visits to the doctor or dentist can be an autonomy minefield. But even ostensibly more innocuous activities, such as expressing affection for a child or asking them to express their affection for others can send the wrong messages. Starting with the principle of bodily autonomy in mind means taking more time and care to explain to children why some things might be necessary, taking the time to understand why they may not want certain things, and finding creative solutions where there is conflict.

We also need to recognize that there are structural issues that prevent parents and caregivers from doing these things. Busy schedules and stressful lives do not always leave us enough time to give children the care and attention they deserve. Social structures and institutions of the state do not always look kindly on parents who give their children autonomy in clothing choices—especially if those parents and children are members of marginalized groups. Formal education is frequently structured in ways that severely limit autonomy, and parents and caregivers have to find ways to counteract or compromise with that. A true consent culture would seek to address the root causes of these issues and enable parents, caregivers, and communities more generally to care for children in ways that foster a strong sense of bodily autonomy.[12]

Our formal education systems also need to address consent. Compulsory, comprehensive, and inclusive sex and relationships education at all levels that not only covers but also centers consent is only a starting point here. We also need to interrogate how the structures of our educational systems impact individual autonomy, and how gendered differences in the treatment of children and young people in schools may reproduce rape culture. Common pedagogical practices such as assigned seating (and especially "boy, girl" seating, which assumes that girls will exert a moderating influence on boys' behavior) potentially force children into close contact with others whom they would prefer not to associate with, and they reproduce cultural practices that make women and girls responsible for the behavior of men and boys. School uniforms and dress codes similarly remove children's autonomy and limit their ability for self-expression. Challenging and reforming these structures will take time but is vital for creating a culture of consent.

Beyond everyday cultural practices, popular culture is a key vehicle for reproducing ideas about gender, sexuality, and consent, and therefore it, too, has a key role to play in dismantling rape culture and creating a culture of consent. The revelation that propelled the #MeToo movement to mainstream awareness was the sheer number and severity of sexual assault allegations against the Hollywood producer Harvey Weinstein. This was then compounded by similar allegations against a number of other high-profile figures within the entertainment industry, in turn reinforcing that those who produce our mainstream popular culture are steeped in rape culture, and are in fact frequently themselves perpetrators of sexual violence. We need to examine who produces our culture, and look for and reward more diversity, both behind the scenes and on screen or page. Allowing a variety of experiences and viewpoints to be represented in our mainstream culture gives us a much better chance to explore issues of consent in positive and constructive ways.

One of the most important contributions popular culture can make toward a culture of consent is to give us the social scripts that normalize everyday consent-centric interactions: show parents respecting children's bodily autonomy, or friends offering hugs (but not imposing them on each other). Another is to help us rewrite the dominant sexual script by introducing more variety in the way sex is depicted: include more queer people, show more consent negotiation (and consent withdrawal being respected), find ways to challenge the privileged position of penile-vaginal intercourse in our society—and do it in content aimed at all ages, from Disney blockbusters and PG-13 fade-to-black scenes to hardcore pornography. (If *Deadpool* can do it, others can too!)

These are just some of the first steps toward the kind of cultural transformation we need to dismantle rape culture and create a culture of consent. Together with legal reform and support for victims and survivors, they are a start. But we also need to understand how rape culture is embedded in our wider social and power structures, and therefore where resistance to such change may come from and what it may look like.

Beyond everyday cultural practices, popular culture is a key vehicle for reproducing ideas about gender, sexuality, and consent, and therefore it, too, has a key role to play in dismantling rape culture and creating a culture of consent.

## Resistance to Change

Rape culture is part of a wider set of systems of power and oppression. Patriarchy, capitalism, racism, ableism, cis- and heteronormativity, and compulsory sexuality—and the people who benefit from these systems—all rely on a culture that obscures and dismisses boundary violations, that uses sexuality to construct some of us as less or more human than others, that blames and re-traumatizes the victims of sexual violence while enabling perpetrators. Oppressive systems have a long history of resisting change, and a range of tactics available to them for doing so.

Historically, rape culture has been reproduced through the silencing and blaming of victims, but also through some of our culture's dominant ideas about gender and sex, such as the male sexual drive discourse or compulsory sexuality. The more a system of oppression can convince us that its operation is "natural," the more invisible it becomes and less resistance it is likely to encounter. It has taken decades of persistent feminist campaigning, activism, and knowledge development to get to a point where we now recognize the ubiquity of sexual violence and the cultural environment that enables it. The #MeToo movement, and the public attention it has gained, is the current high-water mark of these activities.

So when silencing and normalization of rape culture no longer work, what other tactics for resisting change are we likely to see employed against the #MeToo movement or against anyone seeking to build a culture of consent? Both feminist and other liberation movements are familiar with tactics such as backlash, co-optation, and placation. We are already seeing signs of these, as those who benefit from rape culture seek to find a way to limit the effects of any demands for change.

Anti-feminist backlash is of course nothing new. Every big demand that women's movements have made, from the vote to workplace and reproductive rights, has seen backlash ranging from ridicule to violence. Backlash can come from the state (think for instance of the incarceration and force-feeding of suffragettes) as well as from non-state groups and individuals (like organized anti-suffrage movements).

Backlash against campaigns on issues of sexual violence also has a long history that predates the recent rise of the #MeToo movement. In 1991, for instance, a feminist group at Antioch College in the United States succeeded in raising awareness of issues of campus rape and date rape. In response, the college changed its policy and student handbook to better protect students. It could discipline and expel students who violated or sexually assaulted other students, and its definition of sexual assault focused specifically on continuous verbal consent: as intimacy progressed, partners were obliged to verbally ensure consent was still present.

As media picked up the news of the policy, it became a topic of national conversation in the United States in the early 1990s.[13] The vast majority of mainstream opinions were extremely negative, as seen for instance in the 1993 *Saturday Night Live* sketch "Is It Date Rape?," which features, among other things, a male student exaggeratedly asking a female student if it is OK to compliment her on her halter top, kiss her on the mouth, or touch her buttocks.[14] This and other commentary on Antioch's policy are examples of backlash through ridicule. They suggested that a focus on consent in sexual interactions was an unrealistic expectation, that verbally checking for consent would "ruin the mood" and make sex less spontaneous or even less "natural."

While mainstream media has not been quite so crass in the wake of the #MeToo campaign, the underlying discourse of ridicule that constructs consent negotiation as legalistic, too complex, or sucking all the fun out of sex has indeed been a staple of more recent commentators' repertoire. As tapes of then-candidate Donald Trump boasting of grabbing women "by the pussy" were made public leading up to the 2016 US presidential election, US talk radio host Rush Limbaugh produced a five-minute diatribe ridiculing the notion of consent as the arbiter of what was permissible in sexual behavior,[15] and referring to anyone who agreed with this view as the "rape police." There has also been an outbreak of male celebrities asking if they are allowed to flirt anymore, or suggesting that drawing attention to the pervasive nature of sexual violence is "criminalizing courtship."[16]

But the current wave of backlash goes beyond ridicule. A number of powerful men in business and politics, including US vice president Mike Pence, have indicated that they will not take one-on-one meetings with women, lest they be accused of sexual harassment.[17] The subtext here is clear: if women continue to make trouble about this, they will face consequences for their careers and livelihoods. And then there is, of course, the appointment of Brett Kavanaugh to the United States Supreme Court, despite Dr. Christine Blasey Ford's testimony under oath accusing him of attempted rape. This is backlash from the highest levels of the state itself. So, although the media backlash against #MeToo is in some ways more subtle than that against Antioch College's sexual offense prevention program, it is very much still there, still seeking to reproduce rape culture in the same ways, with added help from the state.

Co-optation is another strategy that systems of oppression frequently employ against the demands of liberation movements. Co-optation involves accepting some of the demands for change, or even elevating certain individuals from within liberation movements, while using them to further other agendas or even undermine more radical calls for action. Practices like greenwashing (corporations or governments claiming to be environmentally friendly in marketing or policy materials while engaging in environmentally destructive practices) or pinkwashing (claiming to be LGBT-friendly, or using discourses around LGBT rights to justify oppressing other groups) are examples of this strategy.

Pinkwashing can, for instance, involve pitting the rights of LGBT people against those of ethnic and religious minorities. Countries like the Netherlands that historically have prided themselves on their openness and tolerance of sexual minorities, have come under critique for using that tolerance as a way to justify the exclusion of non-white or Muslim migrants on the spurious grounds of a lack of shared values. And while LGBT rights campaigns, such as those for marriage equality, have seen some success across a number of Western jurisdictions, issues that affect more vulnerable queer people, such as poverty, racism, transphobia, and youth homelessness, are not tackled by states that claim to be LGBT-friendly. So by acquiescing to a limited set of demands for change, states have co-opted LGBT rights campaigns in ways that both continue to oppress queer people and reproduce other forms of oppression such as racism and Islamophobia.[18]

Similarly, we are already beginning to see the co-optation of the #MeToo movement and other campaigns against sexual violence. Both in Europe and in the United States, right-wing politicians have used discourses around protecting women from sexual violence to justify anti-immigrant policies. US president Donald Trump, for instance, has referred to Mexican migrants as "rapists," and a series of sexual assaults at New Year's Eve celebrations in Germany in 2015 fed already smoldering Islamophobic and anti-migrant attitudes, turning them into policy. While the same incidents were a prompt for Germany to change its legal definition of rape to a consent-centric one, they also led to legislation making it easier to deport migrant people. Rather than tackling rape culture and sexual violence, these actions scapegoat minorities and reproduce racial oppression and violence.

There are also indications that the #MeToo movement is being undermined through placation: ensuring that a select few perpetrators face consequences instead of looking at wider, systemic changes. We can see this, for instance, in who exactly is facing consequences for alleged sexual harassment and violence and who is not. Two specific cases that warrant closer examination are that of the US comedian Bill Cosby and the actor Kevin Spacey.

Cosby's conviction in April 2018 on three counts of indecent assault of the same woman was celebrated as the first post-#MeToo case to deliver justice to a victim. Yet the case predates the #MeToo movement. Cosby was charged in 2015 for a sexual assault he committed in 2004. In June 2017, the jury on the original case was deadlocked for five days, leading to a mistrial being declared. In the second trial, conducted in a post-#MeToo environment, the judge allowed five of Cosby's other accusers to testify, and these testimonies are credited with significantly contributing to the conviction. To an extent, this does demonstrate a change in public perception of sexual violence, yet it is also notable that it took six women testifying, with countless others speaking out publicly, to secure this one conviction.

The other prominent figure to have faced definite consequences as a result of sexual assault allegations at the time of writing is Kevin Spacey. The actor Anthony Rapp accused Spacey of sexually assaulting him when Rapp was 14. Spacey unsuccessfully attempted to deflect the allegations by coming out as gay. He was dropped almost immediately from his starring role in Netflix's already-flagging original series *House of Cards* and has been nearly universally condemned by the media.

It is interesting that the two men for whom post-#MeToo justice (in one case through the legal system, in the other through severe career consequences) has been swift are a black man and a gay man. At the same time, Johnny Depp, against whom there are credible and corroborated allegations of domestic violence, continues to be cast in high-profile roles and be used in advertising by corporations such as Warner Bros., Disney, and Dior. And away from Hollywood, Brett Kavanaugh has been appointed to the United States Supreme Court despite equally credible allegations of attempted rape.

This is not to say that Cosby and Spacey should not have suffered consequences for their actions—they absolutely should. Yet given the enormous and growing list of men accused of sexual misconduct just within the entertainment industry, it is notable that the meting out of consequences appears to be reproducing patterns of privilege and oppression. The danger here is that rather than radical, systemic change and a dismantling of rape culture, all we will get is a few heads on platters, in the hope that we will go away.

Some feminist, liberal, and left-wing commentators have also suggested that the #MeToo movement is leading to a sex panic. They raise two key concerns. The first is that a focus on sexual violence may contribute to an atmosphere where sex is increasingly policed, enabling more reactionary and conservative ideas about sex to thrive while having an oppressive effect on queer people and non-normative sexual practices. The second concern is that in dealing with allegations of sexual violence and misconduct, due process and the law seem to have been circumvented in a number of cases—for instance, in Kevin Spacey's—with alleged perpetrators being suspended or fired from their jobs.[19]

Yet in both cases, these are not really problems with raising awareness of and demanding justice for sexual violence. Rather, they are expressions of resistance to change, and structural issues within the criminal justice system and our social and cultural attitudes to sexual violence. Using the #MeToo movement to police queer and non-normative sex and sexualities would be an example of co-optation, and is definitely an issue we need to remain vigilant for. As to due process and the law, even commentators wary of circumventing it, like Masha Gessen, admit that the law does not treat sexual violence in the same way as other crimes, and that the standard of proof in sexual violence cases is effectively higher. We need to be wary of holding up the law as the ultimate arbiter of sexual violence and consent. Here, a focus on supporting survivors and working toward long-term cultural change, while de-centering the law and looking toward transformative justice, would arguably be better approaches.

**Where Next?**

The #MeToo movement is an expression of momentum gathered through decades of feminist activism. It has brought to public attention the pervasiveness of sexual violence, and how our culture enables and reproduces such violence on a daily basis. At the same time, it, and other feminist activism over the years, has pointed toward what a culture of consent might look like and highlighted the need for cultural and legal reform, as well as support for victims and survivors of sexual violence.

Yet we are also already seeing signs of resistance against #MeToo and other attempts to build a culture of consent from those who benefit from rape culture. Backlash, co-optation, and placation are all at work, derailing calls for the dismantling of rape culture and a centering of consent, using sexual violence as a pretext to reproduce other forms of oppression, and finding ways to shore up the discourses and social relations that rape culture is built on.

Social change is rarely as radical as those who initiate it would like it to be. Systems of power are difficult to dismantle, and it takes time—sometimes centuries—to do so. Progress is rarely linear, and setbacks are inevitable. More likely than not, the #MeToo movement will make some headway in some areas, but it will also be accommodated in ways that do not lead to the radical, systemic, structural transformation a true culture of consent would require. But the value of making sexual violence, consent, and issues of power a conversation we are all having, rather than one that is happening in activist groups and niche corners of the internet alone, cannot be underestimated. And while social change is slow, it is not impossible. It requires persistence, celebrating small victories, keeping an eye on the end goal. It requires vigilance against the ways our movement can be derailed, co-opted, or placated before we reach that end goal. And it requires us all to practice a culture of consent at every opportunity in our own day-to-day lives.

# GLOSSARY

**Aromantic**

A person who is aromantic does not experience romantic attraction to others; the opposite of aromantic is alloromantic. Aromanticism is a spectrum, so some people on it may experience romantic attraction less frequently or in different ways than alloromantic people. Distinguishing between different types of attraction (for instance sexual, romantic, aesthetic) is a key contribution of the asexual and aromantic communities toward the understanding of sexuality. Romantic and sexual attractions do not necessarily have to be correlated and a person may experience one or the other or both.

**Asexual**

A person who is asexual does not experience sexual attraction to others. Like aromanticism, asexuality is a spectrum. Asexual people's experiences and attitudes to sex vary. The opposite of asexual is allosexual.

**Cisgender**

The term "cisgender" relates to someone whose gender is the same as the one they were assigned at birth.

**Cisnormativity**

Cisnormativity is the assumption that everyone is cisgender. It underlies a range of social structures and cultural practices.

**Consent**

In the context of sex, consent is the freely given agreement to engage in sexual activities with another person or people.

**Heteronormativity**

Heteronormativity is the assumption that everyone is heterosexual. It underlies a range of social structures and cultural practices.

**Non-binary**

A non-binary person is someone whose gender is either between the two extremes of "man" and "woman," or entirely beyond the binary gender spectrum.

Some examples of non-binary genders include genderfluid, genderqueer, demigirl, demiboy, agender, bigender, neutrois, and non-binary itself. Non-binary people may or may not feel that they are part of a wider transgender community.

**Patriarchy**
Patriarchy is a system of social organization in which men predominantly wield power, and women and people of other genders are marginalized and oppressed.

**Queer**
Queer is used as an umbrella term for gender and sexual minorities, including (but not limited to) people who are gay, lesbian, bisexual, pansexual, asexual, aromantic, intersex, or transgender. Some individuals also use "queer" to describe their own gender and/or sexual orientation.

**Rape**
Legal definitions of rape tend to focus on penetrative intercourse. In some jurisdictions, penetrative intercourse without consent is sufficient to be counted as rape, whereas in others additional factors, such as the use of force or threats, are taken into account before an act counts as rape.

**Rape culture or rape-supportive culture**
Rape culture is a cultural environment (a set of beliefs, practices, and attitudes) that enables sexual violence to thrive. Elements of rape culture may include rape myths and victim blaming as well as more subtle and insidious beliefs and practices.

**Sexual violence**
A wider concept than rape, sexual violence encompasses any sexual act performed without a person's consent (though legal definitions also vary by jurisdiction).

**Transgender**
A transgender person is someone whose gender is not the same as the one they were assigned at birth.

# FURTHER READING

Attwood, Feona. "Reading Porn: The Paradigm Shift in Pornography Research." *Sexualities* 5, no. 1 (2002).

AVEN, the Asexuality Visibility and Education Network. https://asexuality .org/.

Barker, Meg-John, Rosalind Gill, and Laura Harvey. *Mediated Intimacy: Sex Advice in Media Culture* (Cambridge: Polity, 2018).

Crenshaw, Kimberlé. "Mapping the Margins: Intersectionality, Identity, Politics, and Violence against Women of Color." *Stanford Law Review* 43, no. 6 (1991).

Deer, Sarah. "Decolonizing Rape Law: A Native Feminist Synthesis of Safety and Sovereignty," *Wičazo Ša Review* 24, no. 2 (2009).

Downing, Lisa. "What Is 'Sex Critical' and Why Should We Care About It?" *Sex Critical* (blog), July 27, 2012, http://sexcritical.co.uk/2012/07/27/what -is-sex-critical-and-why-should-we-care-about-it/.

Engle, Gigi. "A Guide to Anal Sex." *Teen Vogue*, May 16, 2018. https://www .teenvogue.com/story/anal-sex-what-you-need-to-know.

Friedman, Jaclyn, and Jessica Valenti, eds. *Yes Means Yes: Visions of Female Sexual Power and a World without Rape* (Berkeley: Seal Press, 2008).

Gavey, Nicola. *Just Sex?: The Cultural Scaffolding of Rape* (Abingdon, UK: Routledge, 2013).

Gupta, Kristina. "Compulsory Sexuality: Evaluating an Emerging Concept." *Signs: Journal of Women in Culture and Society* 41, no. 1 (2015).

Hancock, Justin, and Meg-John Barker. *Enjoy Sex (How, When and If You Want To): A Practical and Inclusive Guide* (London: Icon Books, 2017).

Harrad, Kate, ed. *Purple Prose: Bisexuality in Britain* (Portland, OR: Thorntree Press, 2016).

Jo. "Sex Positivity, Compulsory Sexuality, and Intersecting Identities." *A Life Unexamined* (blog), June 27, 2012. https://alifeunexamined.wordpress

.com/2012/06/27/sex-positivity-compulsory-sexuality-and-intersecting -identities/.

Karnythia. "On Consent, Sex-Positivity, & Cultures of Color after Colonization." *The Angry Black Woman* (blog), August 25, 2011. http://theangryblack woman.com/2011/08/25/on-consent-sex-positivity-cultures-of-color-after -colonization/.

Kitzinger, Celia, and Hannah Frith. "Just Say No? The Use of Conversation Analysis in Developing a Feminist Perspective on Sexual Refusal." *Discourse & Society* 10 (1999).

Philly's Pissed. *Learning Good Consent*. https://www.phillyspissed.net/sites/ default/files/learning%20good%20consent2.pdf.

McRuer, Robert. "Compulsory Able-Bodiedness and Queer/Disabled Existence." In *The Disability Studies Reader* (2nd ed.), ed. Lennard J. Davis, 301–308 (Abingdon, UK: Taylor & Francis, 2006).

*Meg-John and Justin.* Podcast website. https://megjohnandjustin.com/.

Pateman, Carole. "Women and Consent." *Political Theory* 8, no. 2 (1980).

Pausé, Cat. "Human Nature: On Fat Sexual Identity and Agency." In *Fat Sex: New Directions in Theory and Activism*, eds. Helen Hester and Caroline Walters, 37–48 (Farnham, UK: Ashgate, 2015).

Smart, Carol. *Feminism and the Power of Law* (London: Routledge, 1989).

Tellier, Stephanie. "Advancing the Discourse: Disability and BDSM." *Sexuality and Disability* 35 (2017).

Temkin, Jennifer, Jacqueline M. Gray, and Jastine Barrett. "Different Functions of Rape Myth Use in Court: Findings from a Trial Observation Study." *Feminist Criminology* 13, no. 2 (2016).

*What About the Rapists? Anarchist Approaches to Crime and Justice.* http:// dysophia.org.uk/wp-content/uploads/2014/09/Dys5-WhatAboutTheRapists Web2.pdf.

# NOTES

## Chapter 1

1. Sylvia Walby and Jonathan Allen, *Domestic Violence, Sexual Assault and Stalking: Findings from the British Crime Survey* (London: Home Office, 2004).

2. Michele Burman and Oona Brooks-Hay, "Victims Are More Willing to Report Rape, So Why Are Conviction Rates Still Woeful?," *The Conversation*, March 8, 2018, https://theconversation.com/victims-are-more-willing-to-report-rape-so-why-are-conviction-rates-still-woeful-92968.

3. Sameena Mulla, *The Violence of Care: Rape Victims, Forensic Nurses, and Sexual Assault Intervention* (New York: New York University Press, 2014).

4. Sue Lees, "Judicial Rape," *Women's Studies International Forum* 16, no. 1 (1993).

5. The feminist writer Michelle Goldberg rightly called out the parallels between Brett Kavanaugh's confirmation and the experience of sexual violation. [Content note: the following quote discusses experiences of sexual violence.] In a *New York Times* opinion piece, she wrote, "In the end, it didn't really matter how many women begged them not to do this, how many times women said slow down, stop, please, no. As of this writing, it seems inevitable that Republicans in the Senate are going to shove Brett Kavanaugh down our throats." See Michelle Goldberg, "A Supreme Violation," *New York Times*, October 4, 2018, https://www.nytimes.com/2018/10/04/opinion/kavanaugh-fbi-supreme-court-republicans.html.

6. See, for instance, Tamar Dina, "The Problem with Consent," *The Coast*, December 14, 2017, https://www.thecoast.ca/halifax/the-problem-with-consent/Content?oid=11456174.

7. Carole Pateman, "Women and Consent," *Political Theory* 8, no. 2 (1980).

## Chapter 2

1. Catharine MacKinnon, *Toward a Feminist Theory of State* (Cambridge, MA: Harvard University Press, 1989), and "Reflections on Sex Equality under Law," *Yale Law Journal* 100, no. 5 (1991).

2. Lois Pineau, "Date Rape: A Feminist Analysis," *Law and Philosophy* 8, no. 2 (1989).

3. For an outline and partial critique of both the "no means no" and "yes means yes" models of consent, see Michelle J. Anderson, "Negotiating Sex," *Southern California Law Review* 41 (2005).

4. The term "sex-critical" was coined by Lisa Downing, and has a wider scope than just consent negotiation. For an accessible introduction to it, see Lisa Downing, "What Is 'Sex Critical' and Why Should We Care About It?," *Sex Critical* (blog), July 27, 2012, http://sexcritical.co.uk/2012/07/27/what-is-sex-critical-and-why-should-we-care-about-it/.

5. See Kimberlé Crenshaw, "Mapping the Margins: Intersectionality, Identity, Politics, and Violence against Women of Color," *Stanford Law Review* 43, no. 6 (1991), and Angela Y. Davis, "Rape, Racism, and the Capitalist Setting," *The Black Scholar* 9, no. 7 (1978).

6. For an account of the impact of racial stereotypes and racialized rape myths on black women's experience of sexuality, see Karnythia, "On Consent, Sex-Positivity, & Cultures of Color after Colonization," *The Angry Black Woman* (blog), August 25, 2011, http://theangryblackwoman.com/2011/08/25/on-consent-sex-positivity-cultures-of-color-after-colonization/. For an in-depth critique of the US criminal justice system in relation to sexual violence against indigenous women, see Sarah Deer, "Decolonizing Rape Law: A Native Feminist Synthesis of Safety and Sovereignty," *Wičazo Ša Review* 24, no. 2 (2009). For an account of the impact of legal structures on migrant women's experience of sexual violence, see Miriam Zoila Pérez, "When Sexual Autonomy Isn't Enough: Sexual Violence against Immigrant Women in the United States," in *Yes Means Yes: Visions of Female Sexual Power and a World without Rape*, eds. Jaclyn Friedman and Jessica Valenti (Berkeley, CA: Seal Press, 2008).

7. For an in-depth discussion about what the law does and does not value about human sexuality, as well as suggestions for reform, see Nicola Lacey, *Unspeakable Subjects: Feminist Essays in Legal and Social Theory* (Oxford: Hart, 1998).

8. See United States Department of Justice, "An Updated Definition of Rape," https://www.justice.gov/archives/opa/blog/updated-definition-rape (2012).

9. Amnesty International, "Sex without Consent Is Rape. So Why Do Only Nine European Countries Recognize This?," https://www.amnesty.org/en/latest/campaigns/2018/04/eu-sex-without-consent-is-rape/ (2018).

10. Molly Redden, "'No Doesn't Really Mean No': North Carolina Law Means Women Can't Revoke Consent for Sex," *Guardian*, June 24, 2017, https://www.theguardian.com/us-news/2017/jun/24/north-carolina-rape-legal-loophole-consent-state-v-way.

11. For a detailed analysis of the law's special status in society and what that means for a range of feminist issues, see Carol Smart, *Feminism and the Power of Law* (London: Routledge, 1989).

12. Sue Lees has coined the term "judicial rape" to describe the extent to which the criminal justice system may re-traumatize a rape victim during investigation, evidence collection, and trial in "Judicial Rape," *Women's Studies International Forum* 16, no. 1 (1993). As some examples of this process, Sameena Mulla shows the invasive and traumatic nature of forensic evidence collection (or rape kits) from rape victims in *The Violence of Care: Rape Victims, Forensic Nurses, and Sexual Assault Intervention* (New York: New York University Press, 2014); Susan Estrich shows how rape victims are held to the standard of "utmost resistance" in rape trials in "Rape," *Yale Law Journal* 95 (1986); Susan Ehrlich shows how the adversarial nature of rape trials and the language used by defense lawyers work to shift responsibility from defendants to complainants in *Representing Rape: Language and Sexual Consent* (New York: Routledge, 2003); and Jennifer Temkin's research team demonstrates in detail how rape myths are leveraged by defense lawyers in courtrooms, and how they go unchallenged by either the prosecution or judges in "Different Functions of Rape Myth Use in Court: Findings from a Trial Observation Study," *Feminist Criminology* 13, no. 2 (2016).

13. See Deer, "Decolonizing," and A. Big Country, "Non-Natives Are Using This Tribal Law Loophole to Rape Indigenous People," *Wear Your Voice*, October 19, 2016, https://wearyourvoicemag.com/identities/race/tribal-loophole-rapists.

14. Smart, "Feminism."

**Chapter 3**

1. Rockstar Dinosaur Pirate Princess, "Consent: Not Actually That Complicated," http://rockstardinosaurpirateprincess.com/2015/03/02/consent-not-actually-that-complicated/.

2. Meg-John Barker, Rosalind Gill, and Laura Harvey, *Mediated Intimacy: Sex Advice in Media Culture* (Cambridge: Polity, 2018).

3. See for instance Kristen Jozkowski and Zoe D. Peterson, "College Students and Sexual Consent: Unique Insights," *Journal of Sex Research* 50, no. 6 (2013).

4. For an in-depth discussion of the need to normalize asking for consent to touch, both in and outside sexual situations, see Hazel/Cedar Troost, "Reclaiming Touch: Rape Culture, Explicit Verbal Consent, and Body Sovereignty" in *Yes Means Yes: Visions of Female Sexual Power and a World Without Rape*, eds. Jaclyn Friedman and Jessica Valenti (Berkeley, CA: Seal Press, 2008).

5. This is not primarily a self-help or sex advice book, though it seeks to answer some basic questions. For further resources, see, for instance: chapters 14 and 15 in Friedman and Valenti, eds., *Yes Means Yes*; Philly's Pissed, *Learning Good Consent*, https://www.phillyspissed.net/sites/default/files/learning%20

good%20consent2.pdf; Meg-John Barker, *Rewriting the Rules: An Integrative Guide to Love, Sex and Relationships* (Abingdon, UK: Routledge, 2012); Justin Hancock and Meg-John Barker, *Enjoy Sex (How, When and If You Want To): A Practical and Inclusive Guide* (London: Icon Books, 2017); and the *Meg-John and Justin* podcast, https://megjohnandjustin.com/.

6. Jozkowski and Peterson, "College Students."

7. Lois Pineau, "Date Rape: A Feminist Analysis," *Law and Philosophy* 8, no. 2 (1989).

8. Celia Kitzinger and Hannah Frith, "Just Say No? The Use of Conversation Analysis in Developing a Feminist Perspective on Sexual Refusal," *Discourse & Society* 10 (1999).

9. See Regina Respondent and R. Appellant, the 1991 case used as precedent to establish marital rape as an offense in England and Wales, http://www.bailii.org/uk/cases/UKHL/1991/12.html.

10. See Meg-John Barker and Justin Hancock, "7 Tips for a Consensual Hook-up," https://megjohnandjustin.com/sex/7-tips-consensual-hook-up/.

11. For an investigation of the social and material conditions that have led to the rise of chemsex, see Jamie Hakim, "The Rise of Chemsex: Queering Collective Intimacy in Neoliberal London," *Cultural Studies* (2018). For a historical overview of the emergence of chemsex and its public health implications see Kane Race, "'Party and Play': Online Hook-Up Devices and the Emergence of PNP Practices among Gay Men," *Sexualities* 18, no. 3 (2015). For an example of a public health–centric call to action on chemsex, see Hannah McCall, Naomi Adams, and Jamie Willis, "What Is Chemsex and Why Does It Matter?" *British Medical Journal* (2015). For an example of the emerging approach to issues of consent in chemsex, see *Consent and Chemsex: Information for Gay and Bi Men in London*, https://www.survivorsuk.org/wp-content/uploads/2016/11/Consent-and-Chemsex-Advice.pdf.

## Chapter 4

1. For a study of unwanted sex in casual situations, see Laina Y. Bay-Cheng and Rebecca K. Eliseo-Arras, "The Making of Unwanted Sex: Gendered and Neoliberal Norms in College Women's Unwanted Sexual Experiences," *Journal of Sex Research* 45, no. 4 (2008). For a discussion of unwanted sex in long-term relationships see Debra Umberson, Mieke Beth Thomeer, and Amy C. Lodge, "Intimacy and Emotion Work in Lesbian, Gay, and Heterosexual Relationships," *Journal of Marriage and Family* 77, no. 2 (2015).

2. For an accessible introduction to Foucault's ideas, see Lisa Downing, *The Cambridge Introduction to Michel Foucault* (Cambridge: Cambridge University Press, 2008).

3. For a feminist critique and expansion of Foucault's ideas, see Lois McNay, *Foucault and Feminism: Power, Gender and the Self* (Cambridge: Polity, 1992).

4. Susan Bordo, *Unbearable Weight: Feminism, Western Culture, and the Body* (Berkeley: University of California Press, 1993).

5. Nicola Gavey, *Just Sex?: The Cultural Scaffolding of Rape* (Abingdon, UK: Routledge, 2013).

6. Wendy Hollway, *Subjectivity and Method in Psychology* (London: Sage, 1989).

7. For accounts of abuse within evangelical churches, see Becca Andrews, "Evangelical Purity Culture Taught Me to Rationalize My Sexual Assault," *Mother Jones*, September/October 2018, https://www.motherjones.com/politics/2018/08/evangelical-purity-culture-taught-me-to-rationalize-my-sexual-assault/; Becca Andrews, "As a Teen, Emily Joy Was Abused by a Church Youth Leader. Now She's Leading a Movement to Change Evangelical America," *Mother Jones*, May 25, 2018, https://www.motherjones.com/crime-justice/2018/05/evangelical-church-metoo-movement-abuse/; and Morgan Lee, "My Larry Nassar Testimony Went Viral. But There's More to the Gospel Than Forgiveness," *Christianity Today*, January 31, 2018, https://www.christianitytoday.com/ct/2018/january-web-only/rachael-denhollander-larry-nassar-forgiveness-gospel.html.

8. Bay-Cheng and Eliseo-Arras, "The Making of Unwanted Sex."

9. John H. Gagnon and William Simon, *Sexual Conduct: The Social Sources of Human Sexuality* (London: Hutchinson & Co., 1973).

10. Nicola Gavey and Kathryn McPhillips, "Subject to Romance: Heterosexual Passivity as an Obstacle to Women Initiating Condom Use," *Psychology of Women Quarterly* 23, no. 2 (1999).

11. For a discussion of the challenges disabled people face in being recognized as sexual beings and in finding sexual practices outside the dominant script, see Mika Murstein, *I'm a Queerfeminist Cyborg, That's Okay* (Münster, Germany: Edition Assemblage, 2018); Stephanie Tellier, "Advancing the Discourse: Disability and BDSM," *Sexuality and Disability* 35 (2017); and Narelle Warren, Cameron Redpath, and Peter New, "New Sexual Repertoires: Enhancing Sexual Satisfaction for Men Following Non-Traumatic Spinal Cord Injury," *Sexuality and Disability* 36 (2018).

12. See Tatiana Masters et al., "Sexual Scripts among Young Heterosexually Active Men and Women: Continuity and Change," *Journal of Sex Research* 50, no. 5 (2013).

13. The effects of multiple marginalizations (for instance race and gender, in the case of women of color) are known as *intersectional* effects. For an introduction to intersectionality theory and its application to sexual violence against

women of color, see Kimberlé Crenshaw, "Mapping the Margins: Identity Politics, Intersectionality, and Violence against Women of Color," *Stanford Law Review* 43, no. 6 (1991).

14. See for instance AVEN, the Asexuality Visibility and Education Network, https://asexuality.org/.

15. Alex Gabriel, "If Your Sex Ed Doesn't Include Asexuality, You're Going to Have Kids Growing Up Doing Things They Don't Realise They Don't Want to Do" (@AlexGabriel, 2017), https://twitter.com/AlexGabriel/status/883369396399419392.

16. The idea of compulsory sexuality builds on the earlier concept of compulsory *hetero*sexuality coined by Adrienne Rich. In her groundbreaking essay, Rich outlines how the existence of women who love women is erased, invalidated, or regarded as deviant by society, forcing women into unwanted relationships with men. See Adrienne Rich, "Compulsory Heterosexuality and Lesbian Existence," *Signs: Journal of Women in Culture and Society* 5, no. 4 (1980). Disability studies scholar Robert McRuer has also built on this idea to coin the idea of compulsory able-bodiedness, articulating how disabled and queer identities intersect in areas such as sexuality. See Robert McRuer, "Compulsory Able-Bodiedness and Queer/Disabled Existence," *The Disability Studies Reader* (2nd ed.), ed. Lennard J. Davis, 301–308 (Abingdon, UK: Taylor & Francis, 2006).

17. For an overview and evaluation of the concept of compulsory sexuality, see Kristina Gupta, "Compulsory Sexuality: Evaluating an Emerging Concept," *Signs: Journal of Women in Culture and Society* 41, no. 1 (2015). For activist discussions and approaches to the concept, see AVEN https://www.asexuality.org/en/topic/141305-compulsory-sexuality/, and Jo, "Sex Positivity, Compulsory Sexuality, and Intersecting Identities," *A Life Unexamined* (blog), June 27, 2012, https://alifeunexamined.wordpress.com/2012/06/27/sex-positivity-compulsory-sexuality-and-intersecting-identities/.

18. For a case study of the impact of the desexualization discourse on fat people see Cat Pausé, "Human Nature: On Fat Sexual Identity and Agency," in *Fat Sex: New Directions in Theory and Activism*, eds. Helen Hester and Caroline Walters (Farnham: Ashgate, 2015).

19. Umberson, Thomeer, and Lodge, "Intimacy and Emotion Work."

20. For an account of the effects of hypersexualization on black women, see Samhita Mukhopadhyay, "Trial by Media: Black Female Lasciviousness and the Question of Consent," in *Yes Means Yes: Visions of Female Sexual Power and a World without Rape*, eds. Jaclyn Friedman and Jessica Valenti (Berkeley, CA:

Seal Press, 2008). For explorations of the impact of hypersexualization on bisexual people see Surya Monro, *Bisexuality: Identities, Politics, and Theories* (Basingstoke, UK: Palgrave Macmillan, 2015), and Kate Harrad, ed., *Purple Prose: Bisexuality in Britain* (Portland, OR: Thorntree Press, 2016). For a discussion of the history and effects of the hypersexualization of black men, see Akala, *Natives: Race and Class in the Ruins of Empire* (London: Two Roads, 2018).

21. See for instance Catharine MacKinnon, "Reflections on Sex Equality under Law," *Yale Law Journal* 100, no. 5 (1991).

22. See for instance Jennifer Nedelsky, "Reconceiving Autonomy: Sources, Thoughts and Possibilities," *Yale Journal of Law & Feminism* 1 (1989).

**Chapter 5**

1. See "Heads or Tails?—What Young People Are Telling Us about SRE," Sex Education Forum, http://www.sexeducationforum.org.uk/resources/evidence/heads-or-tails-what-young-people-are-telling-us-about-sre.

2. See "SRE—The Evidence," Sex Education Forum, http://www.sexeducationforum.org.uk/sites/default/files/field/attachment/SRE%20-%20the%20evidence%20-%20March%202015.pdf.

3. See "Parents and SRE—A Sex Education Forum Evidence Briefing," Sex Education Forum, http://www.sexeducationforum.org.uk/sites/default/files/field/attachment/SRE%20and%20parents%20-%20evidence%20-%202011.pdf.

4. See Marla E. Eisenberg et al., "Parents' Beliefs about Condoms and Oral Contraceptives: Are They Medically Accurate?" *Perspectives on Sexual and Reproductive Health* 36, no. 16 (2004).

5. See, for instance, "Why 'Baby It's Cold Outside' Should Be Retired," https://www.youtube.com/watch?v=vOwH8gZ3lTE, for an example of critical engagement with a song, and Amanda Chatel, "11 Movie Scenes That Taught Us Stalking Is Romantic," *Bustle*, February 5, 2016, https://www.bustle.com/articles/138402-11-movie-scenes-that-taught-us-stalking-is-romantic, for feminist critiques of stalking behavior in films.

6. For a collection of arguments in this tradition see Catherine Itzin, ed., *Pornography: Women, Violence and Civil Liberties* (Oxford: Oxford University Press, 1992).

7. For a critique of early radical feminist arguments on pornography and an overview of empirical evidence see Lynne Segal, "Does Pornography Cause Violence? A Search for Evidence," in *Dirty Looks: Women, Pornography, Power*, eds. Pamela Church Gibson and Roma Gibson (London: BFI, 1993).

8. For an example of a campaign centered on the alleged effects of online pornography on young people, see Culture Reframed: https://www.culturere framed.org/.

9. See Feona Attwood, "Reading Porn: The Paradigm Shift in Pornography Research," *Sexualities* 5, no. 1 (2002).

10. See for instance Ethical Porn, a website and community dedicated to discussing and developing the idea of ethics in pornography production and representation, with an explicit focus on consent: http://ethical.porn/.

11. Ingrid Ryberg, "Carnal Fantasizing: Embodied Spectatorship of Queer, Feminist and Lesbian Pornography," *Porn Studies* 2, no. 2–3 (2015).

12. Rachael Liberman, "'It's a Really Great Tool': Feminist Pornography and the Promotion of Sexual Subjectivity," *Porn Studies* 2, no. 2–3 (2015).

13. Cat Pausé, "Human Nature: On Fat Sexual Identity and Agency," in *Fat Sex: New Directions in Theory and Activism*, eds. Helen Hester and Caroline Walters (Farnham, UK: Ashgate, 2015).

14. For an account of the impact of extreme pornography legislation on independent queer and feminist producers, see Pandora/Blake, "Video Blog about UK Porn Censorship," http://pandorablake.com/blog/2015/1/video-blog-uk -porn-censorship.

15. See Gigi Engle, "A Guide to Anal Sex," *Teen Vogue*, May 16, 2018, https:// www.teenvogue.com/story/anal-sex-what-you-need-to-know.

16. See Tania Modleski, *Loving with a Vengeance: Mass Produced Fantasies for Women* (London: Routledge, 2008) and Janice A. Radway, *Reading the Romance: Women, Patriarchy, and Popular Literature* (Chapel Hill: University of North Carolina Press, 1984).

17. For reinterpretations of the romance novel genre see Pamela Regis, *A Natural History of the Romance Novel* (Philadelphia: University of Pennsylvania Press, 2013) and Catherine M. Roach, *Happily Ever After. The Romance Story in Popular Culture* (Bloomington: Indiana University Press, 2016).

18. Romance reading as a social and communal activity is in fact a major focus of Radway's pioneering study. See Radway, "Reading the Romance."

19. For romance authors' perspectives, see Kelly Faircloth, "The Romance Novelist's Guide to Hot Consent," *Jezebel*, February 14, 2018, https://jezebel .com/the-romance-novelists-guide-to-hot-consent-1822991922.

20. Meg-John Barker, Rosalind Gill, and Laura Harvey. *Mediated Intimacy: Sex Advice in Media Culture* (Cambridge: Polity, 2018).

21. See Markham Heid, "Is Blue Balls Real—How to Cure Blue Balls," in *Men's Health*, May 7, 2018, https://www.menshealth.com/sex-women/a19534594/ science-blue-balls/.

22.  For an example of a review by a white critic, see Casey Cipriani, "'Moana's' Lack of a Love Interest Is Both Revolutionary & Totally No Big Deal," *Bustle*, November 23, 2016, https://www.bustle.com/articles/196517-moanas-lack -of-a-love-interest-is-both-revolutionary-totally-no-big-deal. For reviews by critics of color, see Celeste Noelani and Jeanne, "Moana," *Strange Horizons*, January 30, 2017, http://strangehorizons.com/non-fiction/reviews/moana/, and Jeanne, "Can we stop this bullshit where we assume, without nuanced analysis, that a story with no romance is more feminist than Romance? It's not." (@fangirlJeanne, 2016), https://twitter.com/fangirlJeanne/status/ 807625593344770052.

23.  Patricia Hill Collins, *Black Feminist Thought: Knowledge, Consciousness, and the Politics of Empowerment* (London: Routledge, 1990).

**Chapter 6**

1.  Wendy Hollway, *Subjectivity and Method in Psychology* (London: Sage, 1989).

2.  See, for instance, some of the accounts in Philly's Pissed, *Learning Good Consent*, https://www.phillyspissed.net/sites/default/files/learning%20good %20consent2.pdf.

3.  Michele Burman and Oona Brooks-Hay, "Victims Are More Willing to Report Rape, So Why Are Conviction Rates Still Woeful?," *The Conversation*, March 8, 2018, https://theconversation.com/victims-are-more-willing-to -report-rape-so-why-are-conviction-rates-still-woeful-92968.

4.  Carol Smart, *Feminism and the Power of Law* (London: Routledge, 1989).

5.  Angela Y. Davis, "Rape, Racism and the Capitalist Setting," *The Black Scholar* 9, no. 7 (1978).

6.  See *What about the Rapists? Anarchist Approaches to Crime and Justice*, http:// dysophia.org.uk/wp-content/uploads/2014/09/Dys5-WhatAboutTheRapists Web2.pdf.

7.  See Philly's Pissed, *Learning Good Consent*, https://www.phillyspissed.net/ sites/default/files/learning%20good%20consent2.pdf.

8.  Meg-John Barker, Rosalind Gill, and Laura Harvey, *Mediated Intimacy: Sex Advice in Media Culture* (Cambridge: Polity, 2018).

9.  See Meg-John Barker, "Consent Is a Grey Area? A Comparison of Under-standings of Consent in *50 Shades of Grey* and on the BDSM Blogosphere," *Sexualities* 16, no. 8 (2013).

10.  [Content note: descriptions of abuse and victim blaming in both pieces.] See for instance Cliff Pervocracy, "The Scene Is Not Safe," https://pervocracy .blogspot.com/2012/04/scene-is-not-safe.html; Thomas, "There's a War On Part 3: A Fungus Among Us," *Yes Means Yes*, https://yesmeansyesblog.word press.com/2012/04/20/theres-a-war-on-part-3-a-fungus-among-us/.

11. Pervocracy, "The Scene."

12. See for instance Cliff Pervocracy's series of commentary posts, https://pervocracy.blogspot.com/p/fifty-shades-of-grey-index.html.

13. For demographic data on the fanfiction community generated by the community itself see centrumlumina, *The AO3 Census*, http://centrumlumina.tumblr.com/post/63208278796/ao3-census-masterpost.

14. About a third of fanfiction stories posted on the Archive of Our Own (a fan-owned, fan-run website that hosts over four million works of fanfiction) is rated Mature or Explicit. About half of the works on the Archive of Our Own focus on same-gender relationships, with the vast majority of those (45 percent of total works) focusing on relationships between men. See destinationtoast, "Popularity, Word Count and Ratings on AO3," http://destinationtoast.tumblr.com/post/65586599242/popularity-word-count-and-ratings-on-ao3-faq, and destinationtoast, "Because I was curious about the breakdown of fic on AO3," http://destinationtoast.tumblr.com/post/50201718171/because-i-was-curious-about-the-breakdown-of.

15. See Rebecca Tushnet, "Copyright Law, Fan Practices, and the Rights of the Author" in *Fandom: Identities and Communities in a Mediated World,* eds. Jonathan Gray, C. Lee Harrington, and Cornel Sandvoss (New York: New York University Press, 2007), 60–71.

16. For detailed explorations of fanfiction tropes about power differentials, see Milena Popova, "'Dogfuck Rapeworld': Omegaverse Fanfiction as a Critical Tool in Analyzing the Impact of Social Power Structures on Intimate Relationships and Sexual Consent," *Porn Studies* (2018), and Milena Popova, "Rewriting the Romance: Emotion Work and Consent in Arranged Marriage Fanfiction," *Journal of Popular Romance Studies* (2018).

### Chapter 7

1. For Burke's own words, see https://youtu.be/ZF55ItXWjck and https://metoomvmt.org/.

2. See Elizabeth Wagmeister, "How Me Too Founder Tarana Burke Wants to Shift the Movement's Narrative," *Variety*, April 10, 2018, https://variety.com/2018/biz/news/tarana-burke-me-too-founder-sexual-violence-1202748012/, and Tarana Burke, "I've said repeatedly that the *#metooMVMT* is for all of us, including these brave young men who are now coming forward." (@TaranaBurke, 2018), https://twitter.com/TaranaBurke/status/1031498206260150272.

3. Amnesty International, "Sex Without Consent Is Rape. So Why Do Only Nine European Countries Recognize This?" https://www.amnesty.org/en/latest/campaigns/2018/04/eu-sex-without-consent-is-rape/ (2018).

4. Ed O'Loughlin, "Acquittal in Irish Rugby Case Deepens Debate on Sexual Consent," *New York Times*, April 15, 2018, https://www.nytimes.com/2018/04/15/world/europe/ireland-rugby-paddy-jackson-stuart-olding.html.

5. Jennifer Temkin, Jacqueline M. Gray, and Jastine Barrett, "Different Functions of Rape Myth Use in Court: Findings from a Trial Observation Study," *Feminist Criminology* 13, no. 2 (2016).

6. "What Is the Rape Kit Backlog?," *End the Backlog*, http://www.endtheback log.org/backlog/what-rape-kit-backlog.

7. Sameena Mulla, *The Violence of Care: Rape Victims, Forensic Nurses, and Sexual Assault Intervention* (New York: New York University Press, 2014).

8. Galop, "Barriers Faced by LGBT People in Accessing Non-LGBT Domestic Violence Support Services," http://www.galop.org.uk/wp-content/uploads/For-Service-Providers-Barriers.pdf, and Galop, "Myths and Stereotypes about Violence and Abuse in Same-Sex Relationships," http://www.galop.org.uk/wp-content/uploads/For-Service-Providers-Myths.pdf.

9. Elizabeth Kennedy, "Victim Race and Rape," Feminist Sexual Ethics Project, https://www.brandeis.edu/projects/fse/slavery/united-states/slav-us-articles/art-kennedy.pdf.

10. Survivor of Color Prevalence Rates, http://endrapeoncampus.org/new-page-3/.

11. "What Do We Know about the Ethnicity of People Involved in Sexual Offences Against Children?" *Full Fact*, https://fullfact.org/crime/what-do-we-know-about-ethnicity-people-involved-sexual-offences-against-children/.

12. For resources on teaching children bodily autonomy, see "Body Autonomy, Boundaries and Consent," *Peaceful Parent*, https://www.peacefulparent.com/my-body-belongs-to-me/; "Five Ways to Honour Your Child's Body Autonomy," *Lulastic and the Hippyshake*, http://lulastic.co.uk/parenting/five-ways-honour-childs-body-autonomy/; Akilah S. Richards, "3 Mistakes Parents Make When Teaching Consent and Bodily Autonomy—And How to Fix Them," *Everyday Feminism*, April 7, 2016, https://everydayfeminism.com/2016/04/parents-kids-bodily-autonomy/; "Respecting a Child's Right to Say No & Make Choices About Their Own Body," *The Pragmatic Parent,* https://www.thepragmaticparent.com/body-autonomy-and-right-to-say-no/.

13. Nicolaus Mills, "How Antioch College Got Rape Right 20 Years Ago," *The Daily Beast*, December 10, 2014, https://www.thedailybeast.com/how-antioch-college-got-rape-right-20-years-ago.

14. For a full transcript of the sketch, see http://snltranscripts.jt.org/93/93bdaterape.phtml.

15. See The Young Turks, "Rush Limbaugh: Sexual Consent Is Overrated," https://www.youtube.com/watch?v=QGsAXF3uwr8.

16. See for instance Geraldo Rivera, "Sad about @MLauer great guy, highly skilled & empathetic w guests & a real gentleman to my family & me." (@GeraldoRivera, 2017), https://twitter.com/GeraldoRivera/status/93597674 9766205448.

17. Claire Cain Miller, "Unintended Consequences of Sexual Harassment Scandals," *New York Times*, October 9, 2017, https://www.nytimes.com/2017/ 10/09/upshot/as-sexual-harassment-scandals-spook-men-it-can-backfire -for-women.html. Of course the framing here of this phenomenon as an "unintended consequence" rather than part of the backlash against feminist activism in itself helps obscure the issues and reproduce rape culture.

18. For a discussion of the co-optation of LGBT rights campaigns and the development of the concept of homonationalism, see Jasbir Puar, *Terrorist Assemblages: Homonationalism in Queer Times* (Durham, NC: Duke University Press, 2017).

19. Masha Gessen has been particularly outspoken on this issue. See Masha Gessen, "When Does a Watershed Become a Sex Panic?" *New Yorker*, November 14, 2017, https://www.newyorker.com/news/our-columnists/ when-does-a-watershed-become-a-sex-panic; and Masha Gessen, "Sex, Consent, and the Dangers of 'Misplaced Scale'," *New Yorker*, November 27, 2017, https://www.newyorker.com/news/our-columnists/sex-consent-dangers -of-misplaced-scale.

# INDEX

**The MIT Press Essential Knowledge Series**

**MILENA POPOVA** is an independent scholar, activist, and consultant working on culture and sexual consent.